RUSSIAN COOKBOOK

KYRA PETROVSKAYA

DOVER PUBLICATIONS, INC.
New York

Published in Canada by General Publishing Company, Ltd., 30 Lesmill Road, Don Mills, Toronto, Ontario.

This Dover edition, first published in 1992, is an unabridged republication of the work originally published by Prentice-Hall, Inc., Englewood Cliffs, N.J., in 1961 under the title *Kyra's Secrets of Russian Cooking*.

Manufactured in the United States of America
Dover Publications, Inc., 31 East 2nd Street, Mineola, N.Y. 11501

Library of Congress Cataloging-in-Publication Data

Wayne, Kyra Petrovskaya.
    [Kyra's secrets of Russian cooking]
    Russian cookbook / Kyra Petrovskaya.
        p.   cm.
    Originally published: Kyra's secrets of Russian cooking. Englewood Cliffs, N.J. : Prentice-Hall, c1961.
    Includes index.
    ISBN 0-486-27329-6 (pbk.)
    1. Cookery, Russian.   I. Title.
TX723.3.W38   1992
641.5947—dc20   92-10473
                                                                CIP

Table of Contents

SOUPS

FISH

Table of Contents

POULTRY

SAUCES

DESSERTS

RUSSIAN
COOKBOOK

INTRODUCTION

When I started thinking about compiling the many recipes that I had inherited and collected in a book on Russian cooking, I decided to hold as much as possible to traditional Russian dishes only.

The Russians have adopted many wonderful recipes as their own from the French or the Germans and many other nations. These have become very popular in Russian homes and restaurants. But they are not Russian dishes! Thus I had to restrain myself, and mention only a few of these adopted dishes.

Russian food in general is quite rich. Recipes usually call for wholesome ingredients, and with modern developments in food processing provide the means for all kinds of short cuts. For example, throughout the book I have mentioned butter as one of the ingredients. Where margarine and other vegetable shortenings are available and perfected it is permissible to substitute them for the more expensive butter. However, in Russia we always insisted on using unsalted butter. I can almost hear an outburst of indignation from my Russian friends for even suggesting such a substitution!

But this book is not for my Russian friends, who know how to prepare Russian food. This book is for my other friends, who are used to short cuts and who utilize these short cuts with great intelligence.

I have visualized the book as one which might help housewives to vary their daily menus and, especially, help them to serve something unusual while entertaining informally.

Anybody can learn how to cook. The best example of that is my own grandmother, who had to learn how to cook, for the first time in her life, when she was well on in her late fifties. Until then, my grandmother, Baroness Von Haffenberg, had scores of servants and cooks.

Then came the Red revolution and grandmother lost everything—not only her servants, but also her three sons and her husband, who were either killed in the war or executed by Red firing squads. She herself spent a few months in jail, but such is the stamina of truly great spirits that she not only readjusted to the new life of poverty, but made herself learn a trade, taught herself how to cook and, in the end, was able to better her position to such an extent that our little family of three lived just as well as our proletarian neighbors, who had no problems of readjustment from extreme wealth to extreme poverty.

Anybody can learn how to cook. Some of us need help, and I hope this book can provide some assistance. Others, perhaps have inborn genius for cooking.

I can never forget a conversation with one of the genius-type cooks. She was an elderly Russian lady, particularly famous for her little meat pastries *pirozhky*, one of our most beloved national dishes. After finishing the third or fourth helping of this delicious dish, I made my way to the kitchen to thank the cook and to try to obtain from her the recipe of the divine *pirozhky*.

"How do you go about making these wonderful *pirozhky?*" I asked the lady after a short exchange of the usual polite conversation.

"Well . . ." the lady hesitated. "Well, I wash my hands . . . then, I put a clean kerchief on my hair and a clean apron and then . . . well, then I cook." She looked at me with such complete innocence that I knew, at once, that this was exactly how she prepared those *pirozhky!*

But then—she was a genius!

And so—let's wash hands, put on clean kerchiefs and aprons, and let's cook! ! !

DEFINITION OF TERMS

- *Appetizers*—variety bits of food (usually salty or sharp) served before the meal.
- *Aspic*—a meat or fish stock usually prepared with gelatine, served cold, which looks and shakes like jelly. Aspic can be also prepared with fruit or tomato juice.
- *Baste*—to moisten the roasting meat or other food with its own juice or with some other liquid while baking.
- *Batter*—a thin blend of flour and other ingredients.
- *Beat*—to blend thoroughly, using rapid rotary motion.
- *Blanch*—to pour boiling water over a food (usually nuts, like almonds) to remove the skins.
- *Blend*—to mix together several ingredients.
- *Braise*—to cook food by quick searing and then simmering under a lid and over a low fire.
- *Broil*—to cook directly over or under the heat.
- *Brush*—to spread butter or eggs, sauce, etc., thinly over the surface of the food.
- *Caramelize*—to heat sugar in a utensil until it is melted and turned brown. Or to heat food containing sugar until it melts and gives the food caramel flavor.
- *Chop*—to cut into small pieces.
- *Combine*—to mix the ingredients.
- *Cream*—to work butter or other shortening with a utensil or by hand until it is creamy and has the appearance of whipped cream.

7

- *Croutons*—cubes of toasted or fried bread usually served with soup or with vegetables.
- *Cube*—to cut into squares.
- *Dice*—to cut into small cubes.
- *Dissolve*—to melt.
- *Dot*—to place small bits of butter over the surface of food.
- *Dredge*—to coat with sugar or flour or butter.
- *Dust*—to sprinkle slightly with sugar or flour or bread crumbs.
- *Entrée*—the main course of the meal.
- *Fat*—any shortening.
- *Fillet*—boneless cut of any meat or fish or poultry.
- *Flake*—to break up into small pieces.
- *Fold in*—to add carefully any beaten ingredient to another ingredient without an additional beating.
- *Fry*—to cook in fat.
- *Garnish*—to decorate one food with another.
- *Giblets*—liver, heart and gizzards of poultry.
- *Grate*—to use grater to make tiny particles of food.
- *Grind*—to put food through a special grinder.
- *Knead*—work dough with pressing motion of the hands, stretching and folding it, and pressing it again.
- *Marinade*—a mixture of many ingredients in which food is placed to soak to get extra flavor or tenderness.
- *Marinate*—to soak food in spicy mixture of many ingredients or in juices of fruits or vinegar, etc.
- *Mince*—to chop very, very fine.
- *Mousse*—a mixture of whipped ingredients, served cold and very often thickened with gelatine.
- *Pare*—to cut off the outer skin of potatoes or apples, etc.

- *Peel*—to cut off the outer skin of potatoes, apples, bananas, etc.
- *Purée*—to press vegetables or fruits through a fine sieve. Also, soups made with the ingredients forced through a fine sieve.
- *Roast*—to cook slowly in an oven.
- *Roll*—to roll with a rolling pin.
- *Sauté*—to cook in a small amount of fat without letting the food get fried or burned.
- *Scald*—to pour boiling liquid over food or immerse food in a boiling liquid for a very short period.
- *Shred*—to cut food into very thin strips.
- *Shortening*—any fat which can be used in baking.
- *Sift*—to put the dry ingredients, like sugar or flour, through a fine sieve or a special sifter.
- *Simmer*—to cook slowly, just below the boiling point.
- *Skewer*—to pierce the chunks of meat or fish or other food by sharp sticks of metal or wood and to hold the food in shape while cooking.
- *Soak*—to hold food in a liquid for a period of time.
- *Stock*—the liquid resulting from the cooking of fish, meat, fruit or vegetables.
- *Whip*—to beat an ingredient until it is fluffy and is increased in volume.

Appetizers

We, the Russians, like to start our meals with *Zakoosky* or appetizers. The variety of the zakoosky table is endless: cold cuts, cheeses of all kinds and descriptions, black and red caviar, pastries, and so forth. There is no definite rule as to what you may or may not serve as zakoosky. You serve anything which tastes good, and the more of it, the better.

One of the main staples of any well-served zakoosky is herring. We love and serve herring in all forms: marinated, salted, smoked, chopped, in sour cream, in salads.

I am giving here several ways of preparing herring—either as an appetizer, for the zakoosky table or as a main dish (see Fish).

Another of the necessary dishes on any zakoosky table is a salad. While in the Western world salads are usually served either before the main course or immediately after (or sometimes, together with the main course), Russians usually serve salads before the meal, at zakoosky time.

Russians are particularly fond of cooked-vegetable salads, and of so-called *baclazhannaya eekra* (egg-plant caviar).

While partaking of zakoosky, Russians drink vodka.

The correct way to drink vodka is to gulp it down in one swallow; never to sip it.

Vodka is usually served in small tumble-type glasses and it tastes best when it is thoroughly chilled.

Ladies hardly ever drink more than one or two glasses unless they *like* to lose control of their behavior.

Men naturally drink much more, but either sex makes good use of zakoosky before and immediately after each swallow of vodka.

HERRING

One of the traditional Russian dishes to serve as an appetizer before dinner or as an hors d'oeuvre, accompanied by vodka, is herring. The Russians serve herring in many ways—marinated, smoked, chopped, even as a main course, accompanied by hot boiled potatoes.

If the herring is too salty (in some old-type Jewish delicatessen one still can buy an old-fashioned whole salty herring, without any fancy trimmings. They are the best!), you must soak it for a couple of hours in plain water or a weak solution of tea.

If you prefer to clean the herring first, then you can soak the fillets in cold milk. It will give them some extra tenderness.

After two hours of soaking, the herring is ready to be served. Cut it in one-inch-thick pieces, attach the herring's head and tail to the end of the prepared pieces (purely for decorative purposes) and garnish it with any kind of cooked vegetables cut and arranged symmetrically on each side of the herring in some attractive design.

Prepare the following sauce (vinegar sauce):

1 teaspoon sugar	*Mix vinegar with sugar, salt*
2-3 tablespoons vinegar	*and pepper*
1 1/2 tablespoons olive or salad oil	*Add oil. Pour the sauce over the herring*
Salt and pepper according to taste	

Or mustard sauce:

1 cooked egg	*3 tablespoons vinegar*
1 teaspoon mustard	*Salt and pepper according to*
1 teaspoon sugar	*taste*
1 tablespoon salad or olive oil	

Cream the egg yolk with mustard and sugar. Add oil slowly and after oil is absorbed—add vinegar, salt and pepper.

Chop the egg white and add to the sauce. Pour the sauce over the herring and serve immediately.

CHOPPED HERRING

1 herring	*Dash of muscat nut and*
2 tablespoons unsalted butter	*pepper*
1 large tart apple	

Soak the fillets of herring in milk for one or two hours. Chop or put them through a coarse grinder and cream them together with butter. Work over the herring with a wooden spatula or a flat wooden spoon, making it as creamy as possible.

Put the tart apple through a grinder and combine it with the herring mixture.

Sprinkle with a dash of freshly ground pepper and muscat nut.

Serve as a spread for thin crackers or as a party dip.

EGGPLANT CAVIAR

Eggplant "caviar" of course has nothing to do with caviar. It is just a very tasty appetizer which I, like most Russians, can eat and eat and eat, completely ignoring the rest of the dinner.

It is easy to prepare, easy to serve, and easy to keep. If you make too much of it at one time, just put it in a glass jar and stick it in the refrigerator. It will keep for a long time.

1 large eggplant
1 large onion, chopped very fine
1 tomato or 1 small can of tomato paste
1 green pepper, chopped very fine

1 teaspoon vinegar
2 tablespoons (or more if needed) olive or vegetable oil
1 teaspoon powdered sugar
Salt and pepper according to taste

Bake the eggplant. When cool, skin it and chop very fine. Chop onion and pepper and brown them slightly in 1 tablespoon of oil. Add tomato (or paste) and simmer for 3-5 minutes, adding the rest of the oil. Add vinegar, sugar, salt, pepper, and chopped eggplant. Cook very slowly for 20-30 minutes adding a little more oil if necessary, to prevent burning.

Remove from heat and cool. Serve thoroughly chilled as an appetizer with thin slices of pumpernickel bread and fresh unsalted butter.

MARINATED HERRING SALAD "OODOVOLSTVIE TESTYA" (FATHER-IN-LAW'S DELIGHT)

1 whole marinated herring
2 cooked and cooled potatoes
1 large tart apple
1 dill pickle
1 raw onion
1 cooked beet
2 hard-boiled eggs

3 tablespoons salad oil
2 tablespoons vinegar
1 teaspoon French mustard
2 tablespoons chopped pars-
ley or dill
Dash of salt and pepper

Clean and bone the herring, taking off its skin.

Cut into one-inch-thick pieces and arrange them to resemble a whole, uncut fish.

Slice vegetables and the apple, saving the beet slices for decoration of the salad.

Slice the hard-boiled eggs, saving the *whites* for decoration.

Make the following sauce: cream the egg yolks with mustard, a dash of salt and salad oil, adding the oil by small amounts in order to make the sauce quite thick. Add vinegar.

Just before serving, mix the chopped vegetables with the sauce adding one tablespoon of finely chopped onion and parsley. Arrange the vegetables on both sides of the herring and sprinkle the whole dish with the remaining parsley and onion. Decorate the top of the herring with slices of the egg whites and slices of cooked beet, making some attractive design. You may try to cut the beet slices with a cookie cutter, and arranging them inside the egg white rims; or, the other way around, put the white rims on top of the beet slices.

This salad is excellent when served with good, undiluted vodka, thin slices of Russian black bread (or pumpernickel) and fresh, unsalted butter. It goes well with beer, too. Serves four to six.

SALADS

SALAD OLIVIER

There are several versions of this famous salad, created
by the French Chef, M. Olivier, but claimed by the Russians as one of the "Russian" dishes. But we, the Russians,
are known for expropriating someone else's ideas: once the
Russians claimed that baseball was invented by a Russian!

Anyhow, be it Russian or French, the salad Olivier is
superb in any of its many versions, each one of them being
proclaimed as the one and only version.

I won't argue with the authors of the pre-revolutionary
versions. I simply shall contribute one of my own or, to be
precise, the version of the salad Olivier as it is served in
Russia today.

1 boiled chicken, boned   3-4 tablespoons mayonnaise
2-3 boiled potatoes   Salt and pepper according to
2-3 hard-boiled eggs   taste
2-3 small dill pickles

Bone the chicken and slice the meat into thin one-inch-long strips. Slice cooked and cooled potatoes similarly. Take off the skin from dill pickles and slice them in the same way as chicken and potatoes; combine them all together.

Very carefully work in mayonnaise.

Make a mound of this salad, decorating the top and the sides of it with the slices of hard-boiled eggs.

Another way to prepare salad Olivier is to use cold duck instead of chicken. In this case, add a few olives (black or green) to the decoration of your salad.

Still another way is to use cold veal instead of fowl.

And still another variation is to use combination of meats (chicken *and* veal) and 1/2 cup of cooked or canned green peas added to the above-mentioned ingredients. Actually, the last version is the most popular one in Russia today.

FRUIT SALAD "YALTA"

3 apples   1/3 cup mayonnaise
1 pear   1 teaspoon lemon juice
1 orange   1 teaspoon powdered sugar
1 tangerine   5-6 cooked prunes, halved

Wash the fruits and peel the orange and tangerine (save the rind of the orange).

Cut the fruits into elongated cubes, and orange and tangerine into thin round slices. Sprinkle the prepared fruits with powdered sugar.

Combine mayonnaise, lemon juice and a dash of salt.

Just before serving, pour the dressing over the fruits and decorate the top of the salad with halves of the cooked prunes, arranging them in some attractive design together with the narrow strips of the orange rind, sliced paper-thin.

Serve with any main course of meat or fowl or as a completely independent dessert. Serves four to six.

VEGETABLE SALAD "SPRINGTIME"

1 head of crisp lettuce	*2 tomatoes*
2 hard boiled eggs	*1 small bunch of green*
2 small cucumbers (or one	*onions*
large)	*1 cup sour cream*
1 bunch of red radishes	*1 tablespoon vinegar*
1 cooked carrot	*1/2 teaspoon powdered sugar*
2-3 cooked and cooled pota-	*Salt and pepper according to*
toes	*taste*

Wash and cut the head lettuce and pile it in a shape of a mound in the middle of a large salad bowl.

Around the mound arrange slices of carrots, potatoes, tomatoes and radishes, creating some attractive design.

Slice the eggs into thin slices and decorate the top of the mound.

Sprinkle the salad all over with finely chopped green onions, salt and pepper.

Prepare the sauce by combining sour cream and vinegar with sugar and serve it in a separate dish. Or, if you prefer, just before serving the salad, pour the sauce over it. Serves four to six.

HEALTH SALAD A LA KIEV

2 cucumbers (or one if very
  large)
2 raw carrots
2 apples
2 tomatoes
1 small head of Romaine or
  Butter Lettuce

2/3 cup sour cream
1 teaspoon lemon juice
  (freshly squeezed)
1/2 tablespoon sugar
Salt and pepper according to
  taste

Wash cucumbers, carrots and apples and cut them into short sticks.

Select only crisp, healthy leaves of lettuce and cut them into 3-4 pieces each.

Mix sour cream and lemon juice together with sugar, salt and pepper and pour the dressing over the prepared vegetables.

Decorate the top of the salad with tomato slices cut just before serving. Serves four to six.

RADISH SALAD (PO DEREVENSKI)

2 bunches of red radishes
1 hard-boiled egg
2/3 cup sour cream

Salt and pepper according to
  taste

Hard boil 1 egg. When cool, cream the yolk together with sour cream.

Add salt.

Cut radish into thin slices and combine them with the sour cream mixture.

Dice the white of the egg into tiny cubes and sprinkle them over the radishes together with some freshly ground pepper. Serves four to six.

RED CABBAGE SALAD

1 head of red cabbage (1 1/4 pounds)
1/3 cup vinegar
1/2 tablespoon sugar

1 tablespoon salad oil (or olive oil)
Salt and pepper according to taste

There are two ways of preparing the cabbage for this salad which is served as an additional garnish to the main course of meat or game.

1. Cut the head of cabbage into 4 pieces in order to remove the stem. Shred the cabbage, rinse it with boiling water and let it stand under a lid for 20 or 30 minutes. After this time, rinse the cabbage with cold water, squeeze the water out and put the cabbage into a serving salad bowl.

Combine vinegar, sugar and oil and pour the mixture over the cabbage. Let it stand for another 20 or 30 minutes and then serve.

2. The second way to prepare the red cabbage for this salad: instead of rinsing the shredded cabbage with boiling water, sprinkle it liberally with salt and start squeezing it firmly with your fingers until the cabbage becomes soft and begins to discharge dark juice. Then, squeeze the juice out, add the vinegar mixture and within a few minutes the cabbage will assume a bright reddish-purple color.

Serve the red cabbage salad with the main course of meat or fried fish. Serves four to six.

WHITE CABBAGE SALAD

1 head of white cabbage (1 1/4 pounds)
1/3 cup vinegar

1/2 tablespoon sugar
1 tablespoon salad or olive oil

Wash and shred one head of cabbage, sprinkle it generously with salt and begin squeezing it until the cabbage becomes soft. Press the juice out, put the cabbage into a serving salad bowl and pour over it vinegar mixed with sugar and oil. Cover with a lid and let it stand for 30-40 minutes before serving.

There is a second way to prepare this salad:

Put the shredded cabbage into a pot, sprinkle with salt and pour vinegar over it.

Simmer slowly, constantly stirring, until the cabbage becomes soft and seemingly diminishes in quantity.

Cool the cabbage and, just before serving, add to it sugar and oil, mixing it all thoroughly.

Serve with any main course of meat, fish or fowl. Serves four to six.

MEAT SALAD

A wonderful way to utilize a few left-overs of a roast or a ham or a leg of lamb!

1/2 pound of cooked meat (or left-overs)
4-5 cooked and cooled potatoes
2 small cucumbers (or one large)

1 head of crisp lettuce
2/3 cup mayonnaise
1 teaspoon vinegar
Salt and pepper according to taste

Dice the meat into small pieces, saving the most perfect ones for decoration of the salad.

Cut potatoes, lettuce and cucumbers and carefully mix them with the diced meat, shaping the salad into a neat mound, and saving a few perfect slices for later. Combine mayonnaise, salt, pepper and vinegar and pour half of the mixture over the salad.

Decorate the top of the salad with a few perfect pieces of meat, alternating them with round slices of cucumber. Encircle the mound with shredded (thin long slices) lettuce and pour over lettuce the remaining mixture of mayonnaise dressing. This salad makes a wonderful and nourishing luncheon meal! Serves four to six.

SALMON OR STURGEON VINAIGRETTE
(SALAD OF SMOKED FISH AND COOKED POTATOES)

1/2 pound smoked salmon or sturgeon
2-3 boiled potatoes, diced
1 tablespoon capers
1 tablespoon minced onion
1/4 cup sliced olives, black or green or a mixture of both

1 tablespoon minced scallions
1 tablespoon vinegar
2 tablespoons salad oil
1 teaspoon prepared mustard
Pepper

Cut salmon or sturgeon into thickish strips. Mince onions, scallions, very fine. Add capers and sliced olives. Mix with the fish very carefully. Add diced potatoes and mix everything with a fork, taking care not to break the fish pieces. Chill in the refrigerator while preparing the following dressing:

Combine vinegar, salad oil, and prepared mustard. Add pepper (and a dash of salt if the fish is not too salty).

Just before serving, pour the dressing over the vinaigrette but do not stir it in, for it might make the vinaigrette too soggy.

WILD GAME SALAD (OKHOTNICHI)

1 pheasant (or partridge or grouse or wild Cornish hen)
4-5 cooked and cooled potatoes
2 hard-boiled eggs
2 small cucumbers (or 2 dill pickles)
1 head of crisp lettuce
1 apple
2/3 cup mayonnaise
1/2 tablespoon of Worcestershire sauce
1 tablespoon vinegar (or lemon juice)
1/2 teaspoon powdered sugar
Salt and pepper according to taste

Cut the lettuce leaves into 2-3 parts lengthwise and pile them into the middle of the salad bowl, making a mound. Sprinkle with salt and pepper.

Cut the fillet of pheasant (or any other wild game) into long, thin slices and save them for decoration of the salad. Dice the rest of the fowl into small pieces and mix them with the sliced potatoes, cucumbers, apple and one hard-boiled egg. Save a few perfect slices of the vegetables for decorating the top of the salad.

Cut the second hard-boiled egg into neat round slices and save them too for decoration.

Combine mayonnaise, Worcestershire sauce, vinegar (or lemon juice) with powdered sugar and pour half of the mixture over the salad mound.

Decorate the top and the sides of the mound with the best pieces of meat, potatoes, apples, cucumbers and egg, alternating them or, arranging them in a form of the little "bouquets." Pour the remaining mayonnaise dressing over the whole salad just before serving.

Sprinkle the top with a little more salt and some freshly ground pepper.

This *okhotnichi* (or hunters') salad has been a favorite dish of Russian hunters for generations. It is very attractive to look at, very easy to prepare, even for a man, and it provides an easy way to dispose of the hunter's "limit." Serves four to six.

FISH AND TOMATO SALAD
(PO MURMANSKI)

1/2 pound fillet of any cooked or smoked fish
2 firm tomatoes
1 cucumber
3 cooked and cooled potatoes
1/2 head of crisp lettuce
1 dill pickle
2/3 cup mayonnaise

1 tablespoon vinegar
3-4 stacks green onions
5-6 olives (green or black, pitted)
Small jar of red or black caviar
Salt and pepper according to taste

Shred lettuce and arrange it in the salad bowl, making it look like a miniature volcano, with a crater.

Slice tomatoes and cucumber and with them decorate the sides of the "volcano."

Cut fish, potatoes and dill pickle and combine them thoroughly but gently.

Fill the crater of the "volcano" with the fish mixture and, if any of the mixture remains, the slopes of it too.

Combine mayonnaise, vinegar and caviar and spread the mixture gently over the salad.

Chop the green onions and the olives and toss them lightly all over the salad together with some freshly ground pepper.

Do not sprinkle any salt if you have used caviar; however, if you have omitted caviar, sprinkle the salad with some salt. Serves six.

CANNED VEGETABLES AND MEAT SALAD

1/2 pound cooked meat
1/2 cup canned green peas
1/2 cup canned diced beets
1/2 cup canned diced carrots
1/2 cup canned yellow beans
3-4 cooked and cooled pota-
toes
1 cucumber (or 1 dill pickle)

1/2 cup mayonnaise
1 teaspoon powdered sugar
1 teaspoon vinegar (or lemon
juice)
1 teaspoon French type mus-
tard
Salt and pepper according to
taste

Drain the canned vegetables. Dice meat, potatoes and cucumbers and mix them with canned vegetables.

Combine mayonnaise, vinegar (or lemon juice), powdered sugar, mustard, salt and pepper, and mix it thoroughly with the vegetables and meat. Put the salad into refrigerator and let it stand there for 30-40 minutes before serving.

An entire luncheon meal! Serves four to six.

Soups

Some of the Russian soups are so full of all kinds of ingredients that they make perfect one-meal dinners and, like the classic vegetable soup, they improve on the second or third day after their preparation.

Here are a few secrets which might be interesting to you in connection with the preparation of Russian soups.

1. When making a meat stock for any kind of soup, all the basic vegetables—carrots, celery, onions, turnips, etc.—must be slightly browned in butter. This process locks in the vegetable juices and gives the meat stock better color.

2. If you happen to make a beef stock from a chunk of tough meat, you can improve the taste of both—the stock and the meat—by adding vodka to the boiling stock. As soon as the foam forms on the top of the stock, carefully remove the foam, add 2 tablespoons of vodka, and continue to cook

until ready. The odor of vodka will evaporate very quickly but the meat will become tender and tasty.

3. When preparing *borsch*, in order to have rich, purplish color, have ready 2-3 tablespoons of grated raw beets. Add the raw beets to the borsch just before serving, and bring the soup to a quick boil once more.

4. If you are making your own bouillon, to have a beautiful golden color you might use one of these methods of coloring the soup:

    a. Save the outer brown skins of the onions which you used for the soup. Wash and simmer them slowly in a separate small utensil in one cup of meat stock. At the end of cooking of the main soup, strain the liquid of the onion skins and add it to the soup.

    b. Dampen with a little water four tablespoons of sugar and slowly heat it on a small skillet until dark brown. Watch that the sugar doesn't burn. When the sugar turns dark, add 2-3 tablespoons of water, bring to a boil, strain and add to the bouillon. You may add this burnt sugar to your soup just before serving. But don't use this method if you intend to keep your soup for the next day's serving as well. In such case, color only the amount needed for the immediate serving. But you may preserve the burnt sugar water in a tightly closed container for several days, heating it and adding it to the soup just before serving.

5. If you want your bouillon or consommé to be crystal clear, strain it through a fine cheesecloth twice, then, bring bouillon to a boil once more. Slightly beat 2 egg whites and pour them into boiling bouillon. Let boil for 1-2 minutes, then strain once more through a napkin, dampened in cold water.

6. Never throw away the tough, top skin of a smoked ham. Save it for adding little pieces of it to your borsch or *schi.*

No meal is complete in Russia without a huge plate of soup. In many cases the soups are so nourishing and so full of all kinds of vegetables and meats that one can't eat anything else. Particularly when the soups are accompanied by those delicious little pastries filled with meat or cabbage or rice or mushrooms! These little pastries—pirozhki—deserve all the flattering adjectives in every possible language and I only wish that they might become as international as meat and potatoes!

The most famous Russian soup is, of course, borsch. There are several variations of this wonderful soup. A cold beet soup, slightly sweet, served with sour cream, is one of the variations on the theme.

Russian or Ukrainian borsch are served piping hot and made of many other ingredients in addition to the traditional beets, which are used mainly for giving the soup its rich reddish color. I give here several recipes for this tasty and nourishing soup. Don't be frightened by the quantities; this soup becomes even better on the second or third day after its preparation. So, serve just enough for your family and guests and keep the rest in the refrigerator. You may even freeze the soup and use it weeks later!

UKRAINIAN BORSCH

Basically, the Ukrainian Borsch is the same as Russian Borsch. During my youth I spent some weeks among Ukrainian peasants, on a *khootor* (a farm) where I helped my hostess prepare huge meals for her big family and farmhands. The main staple of their diet was borsch, which my hostess cooked almost daily in a pot of at least ten gallons capacity.

At meal time, 12 or 15 of us would sit around this large pot, each with his own wooden spoon, waiting for the head of the family to start. Crossing himself piously several times, the head of the family would dip his spoon into the huge pot. His wife would be the next, and so on down the line to the youngest child. It took me, a city-bred girl, a long time to get used to this manner of eating. I had to overcome a shudder of disgust and nausea to dip my spoon into this communal pot. I had to learn how to hold a piece of bread under my chin, as I saw the peasants do, to catch any drippings from the round, wide spoon, which was too big even for the biggest mouth. I had to learn a lot. But, although the custom of eating from a communal pot was foreign to me, the taste of the borsch wasn't. Like every true Slav, I loved it!

7-8 cups of water
1 1/4 pounds soup meat (or a large ham bone)
3/4 pound beets
1 pound potatoes
1 pound cabbage
2/3 cup tomato paste
2 slices of bacon
1 teaspoon vinegar
2 tablespoons butter
2 medium-sized carrots, sliced
1 medium-sized onion, sliced
1 stalk celery
2 tablespoons flour
1 bay leaf
1 clove of garlic
Salt and pepper according to taste
Fresh dill or parsley, chopped very fine
Heavy sour cream

Make the meat stock. While the meat stock is cooking (1-1 1/2 hours) prepare the following borsch ingredients:

Slowly sauté beets, sliced into long strips, together with chopped bacon and tomato paste for 20-30 minutes. When the beets are soft, add vinegar. If at any time during cooking the beets begin to look dry, or threaten to burn, add some meat stock, one tablespoon at a time.

In a separate skillet, brown slightly in two tablespoons of butter sliced carrots, onion and celery. Sprinkle with flour and shake, so that each piece of vegetable will be covered with flour. Add 2-3 tablespoons of meat stock and bring it all to a quick boil.

When the meat in the main skillet is soft, take it out and strain the stock through a cheesecloth folded several times, or a fine sieve.

Add prepared beets, raw potatoes and cabbage cut in rather large pieces. Cook for 10-15 minutes on a low fire.

Add browned vegetables, bay leaf, salt and pepper, according to taste, and continue to cook slowly until potatoes and cabbage are soft.

Add skinned tomatoes, cut in 6 parts each.

Cut meat into medium-size chunks, rubbing each chunk with a clove of garlic and return meat into borsch, bringing it to a quick boil. Remove from fire and let the borsch stand for 15-20 minutes before serving.

Serve in large soup plates or bowls with one tablespoon or more of heavy sour cream for each serving and a dash of chopped dill or parsley.

VARIATION

Some Ukrainians like to put cut frankfurters, or smoky links, as well into their borsch. For the above-mentioned recipe, you may use 1 pound of frankfurters instead of meat. But in any case, don't forget to use an old ham bone to make the basic stock. During the last 10 minutes of cooking, add cut and slightly browned frankfurters to your borsch and serve a few of them for each plate of borsch. Serves four to six.

RUSSIAN BORSCH

9-10 cups boiling water
2 1/2 pounds soup meat (with a marrow bone if possible. You may also use a left-over bone from a baked ham instead of meat)
2 large carrots, sliced
2 stalks of celery with leaves, sliced
2 onions, sliced
2 bay leaves
8-10 medium-sized beets
1/2 head of medium-sized cabbage, sliced not too fine

8 peppercorns (or freshly ground pepper)
1 tablespoon vinegar
2 cups raw and cut tomatoes (skinned), or you may use instead the same amount of drained canned tomatoes
6 tablespoons butter
1 tablespoon flour
Salt according to taste
Soup cream—to heap in plates when soup is served

Put the washed meat in a large pot with nine cups of boiling water. (Later on you may add the tenth cup of boiling water if the borsch looks too thick. My grandmother always kept a kettle of boiling water on the stove when she was cooking—just in case she needed to add a little water to something, or to melt something over it quickly. Or simply to have a cup of tea while she was cooking!)

Add bay leaves, cabbage, peppercorns and start simmering.

Brown slightly, in 2 tablespoons of butter, cut onions, carrots and celery and add them to the simmering soup.

Peel beets, cut in narrow strips, and simmer them in another pot with vinegar, the rest of the butter, and just enough water to cover the beets.

When the beets are tender, add flour, mix well, and combine with the meat stock, which should be ready whenever the meat becomes tender (it takes less time, of course, if you have used a left-over ham bone). Add cut tomatoes to the meat stock and boil quickly for 8-10 minutes. Take the meat out, cut into serviceable pieces and return them to the soup. Or save the meat for the next day's main dish of cold boiled meat with horse-radish.

Serve borsch very hot in large soup plates or bowls with one tablespoon or more of sour cream for each serving. Serves six.

SAUERKRAUT SOUP (SHCHI)

During the last few decades of the eighteenth century and the first decade of the nineteenth century, the Russian nobility went through a period of infatuation with France and everything French. The noblemen imported their chefs from France and in their attempt to be Francophiles, some of them completely ignored such fine, native dishes as shchi, or sauerkraut soup.

The invasion of Napoleon brought back the popularity of everything Russian. All of a sudden it became very fashionable to speak Russian, to dress in Russian national dress, to eat Russian food and to declare oneself a Francophobe.

Thus, shchi, which had been one of the main staples of the peasants' diet, suddenly found its way to the noblemen's tables.

It has held its place on Russian tables ever since.

1 1/2 pounds sauerkraut	*1 tablespoon tomato puree*
7-8 cups meat stock	*3-4 peppercorns*
2 tablespoons butter	*1 bay leaf*
2 tablespoons flour	*Salt, according to taste*
1 medium-sized onion,	*Sour cream—optional*
* chopped*	

Make a meat stock from any amount of soup meat or bones. Or make the stock from mushrooms if the soup is to be meatless.

Brown chopped onions in butter. Add tomato purée and stir in flour. Add sauerkraut and simmer for 1/2 hour under lid. Add meat stock, peppercorns, bay leaf and salt. Simmer for 1 1/2 hours. Take the meat out and cut into serviceable pieces. Remove the soup from the heat and let it stand for 15-20 minutes before serving.

Put a chunk of meat into every plate and serve with a topping of sour cream if desired.

Shchi tastes even better on the second day, so don't be alarmed if you think that you have made too much of it. Just put it into the refrigerator. It will keep improving in taste for several days!

Variation

You may use canned consommé instead of homemade meat stock. In such case, omit salt, for the canned soups are usually well-spiced. But use the same amount of canned soup, cup for cup, as if you were using the homemade meat stock. Serves four to six.

LAZY SHCHI (LENIVY SHCHI)

This soup was one of my favorite "summer soups" when I was a girl. Lazy shchi got its name from some easy-going person who was too lazy during the summer months to prepare the cabbage in order to have sauerkraut for regular shchi. Sauerkraut shchi was always considered to be strictly a winter soup, for it took a long time for the cabbage to ferment and thus to become sauerkraut. So this happy-go-lucky person created a new soup, using fresh cabbage, which went down easier during the summer than its more filling and much heavier relative.

When I was a girl I spent most of my summers at the State Summer Camps, where the children were required to help the farmers at the near-by collective farms to harvest their crops. We, the children, hated our work at the collectives, particularly those of us who belonged to artistic schools, the Leningrad Ballet School and Leningrad Music School of the Academic Capella. Our feet or our hands were our means of making our living in the future; nevertheless, we too were ordered to work in the fields barefoot, bare-handed, without any tools whatsoever. But we were taught to obey and—we obeyed.

As a result of our work in the fields our camp would receive fresh vegetables or fruits which were always welcome, for we were growing up when food in Russia was scarce and every item of food or clothing was rationed strictly.

On those days when we would receive our "premiums" of

fresh vegetables or fruits, large pots of "summer soup"—lazy shchi—were waiting for us. Exhausted, with cut feet and bleeding hands which prevented us from playing the piano or violin or from dancing "en pointes" for some time, we were rewarded somewhat by this terrific soup, which we consumed in enormous quantities!

True lazy shchi is a vegetarian soup. However, you may experiment with it by adding meat to the recipe or by using canned consommé, as a basic stock.

1 cabbage, shredded not too fine	*1 stalk celery, chopped*
	2 parsnips, chopped
4-5 cups water (you may use more water if the soup looks too thick)	*4 tablespoons butter*
	1 bay leaf
	Sour cream
3-4 potatoes, sliced or diced	*Dash of chopped dill or parsley*
1 small onion, whole	
2-4 tomatoes (optional)	*Salt and pepper, according to taste*
3-4 carrots, sliced	
1 turnip, sliced	

Add cabbage to water and when cabbage begins to turn soft, add parsnips, carrots, turnips, bay leaf and celery. Simmer until tender. Add salt and pepper. 20-30 minutes before serving, add potatoes and continue to cook over slow fire. 3-5 minutes before serving, add tomatoes, which are optional. Take out the bay leaf and the onion, add butter and serve in large soup plates or soup bowls with a heaping spoonful of sour cream for each serving and a dash of finely chopped dill or parsley over it.

If you decide to make a meat stock base for your lazy shchi, use the same ingredients but omit butter. Instead, use

1 1/2 pounds of any soup meat (or bones) with 5 cups of water.

If you use the canned consommé as your stock, go easy on salt, but use 4-5 cups of prepared consommé (or more) to serve as your basic stock.

Serves four to six people and keeps its taste overnight.

DRY MUSHROOM SOUP (GRIBNOI)

In Russia we used to eat this delicious vegetarian soup during the winter, when fresh vegetables were unattainable. It is a very aromatic and very economical soup, made of only three vegetables: mushrooms, onions and potatoes.

4-5 cups of water
1/2 pound dry mushrooms
1 large onion, chopped
5-6 potatoes, quartered

1/4 pound butter
Sour cream (optional)
Salt and pepper, according to taste

Soak washed mushrooms in two cups of water, until they are tripled in size and soft and easy to cut in long strips (or short strips, according to the original size of your mushrooms). Drain the mushrooms, but save the water, in which they were soaking and combine it with the remaining water. Bring to a boil.

Meanwhile, brown the mushrooms slightly in butter and, in another skillet, brown the onions in butter. Combine them and add to the boiling water. Add salt and pepper and potatoes. As soon as the potatoes are soft, add remaining butter. Serve hot, with a heaping tablespoon of sour cream for each plate, or just plain, if you wish. The soup has the most wonderful aroma, and tastes best when freshly prepared. Serves four to six.

KIDNEY SOUP (RASSOLNICK)

1 1/4 beef kidney
6-7 cups water or meat stock
1 medium onion
1 stalk celery
2 teaspoons chopped parsley
2 tablespoons butter
4 medium-sized potatoes
2 large dill-pickled cucumbers

4 leaves spinach
2-3 tablespoons dill-pickle marinade
Sour cream
Salt and pepper, according to taste
Dash of freshly chopped dill or parsley

Wash kidney, cut off the skin and excess of fat. Cut each kidney in 4 parts, put in cold water, and bring to a quick boil. Drain the water, rinse kidney in fresh cold water and then combine with the stock, or water, in which the kidneys are to simmer slowly and under a lid for 1 hour 30 minutes.

Wash and cut onions, celery and two teaspoons of parsley, and brown them slightly in 2 tablespoons of butter.

Cut potatoes and dill-pickled cucumbers and combine them with the browned vegetables.

After one hour and thirty minutes of slowly cooking the kidneys, take them out, strain the stock, put the vegetables in. Simmer for another 25-30 minutes.

5-10 minutes before the end of simmering, add salt and pepper, 4 leaves of spinach, cut in strips and 2-3 tablespoons of dill-pickle juice.

Cut the cooled kidneys into smaller pieces and just before serving, add to the stock.

Serve hot, in large soup plates or bowls, with a heaping of heavy sour cream for each plate. Sprinkle the very top with freshly chopped dill or parsley. Tastes very good the next day, too, but in such case, don't keep the kidneys in the stock overnight. Add them to the reheated stock and bring to a quick boil. Serve at once. Serves four to six.

RASSOLNICK OF CHICKEN

This rassolnick is very good when it is made with an old chicken. Naturally, it can be made with a young chicken, too, but there are so many other wonderful dishes which can be prepared only from young chicken that it is *à propos* to stress the point of the old chicken.

1 stewing chicken
7-8 cups chicken stock
4-5 dill-pickled medium-sized cucumbers
5-6 tablespoons dill-pickled cucumber juice
2 carrots
2 turnips
1 stalk celery
1/2 cup pearl barley or long-grained rice, precooked
1 pound beef or ox kidney
Sour cream
Salt and pepper according to taste

Make chicken stock. When ready, take the chicken out, strain the stock and combine with cucumber juice. Slice cucumbers, carrots, celery, and turnips and cook in a small amount of stock until tender. While the vegetables are cooking, wash the kidneys, cut in medium-sized chunks and bring to a quick boil in a small amount of water. Strain the kidneys, and cut them into smaller pieces. As soon as the vegetables are tender, strain them and add to the stock, together with cooked barley or rice. Bring to a boil and continue to cook slowly for another 25-30 minutes. When about ready to serve, add kidneys and, if you wish, small pieces of boiled chicken. However, if you are an economical type, as I am, save the boiled chicken for the next day, for this soup is so good and tasty that you might even make a whole meal of it, as we often do in Russia. Serves eight.

FISH SOUP (OOKHA)

Ookha, a favorite soup of the peasants, became famous after a Russian poet, Ivan Krilov, wrote a fable about it at the beginning of the nineteenth century. "The Demianova Ookha" became proverbial for its moral—"too much of even something truly good becomes too bad for one's own good."

For ookha, use white-fleshed fish. Use two different kinds of fish, like cod and flounder or haddock and flounder, etc. Some purists use even three different kinds of fish, all in the same soup!

3 pounds white-fleshed fish	*1 bay leaf*
6-7 cups water	*4-6 peppercorns*
1-2 carrots	*2-3 twigs parsley*
1-2 small onions	*Salt and pepper according*
1-2 stalks celery	*to taste*

Trim and clean fish but do not skin or bone it. Slice the vegetables and combine them with water, fish and spices (you may add a tiny dash of nutmeg if you like its flavor).

Bring to a quick boil and then simmer slowly for 1 1/2 or 2 hours. Strain through a very fine sieve or cheesecloth folded several times. The Russian peasants don't strain the soup. They like their ookha thick and they eat all the cooked pieces of fish together with the vegetables. So—you may try it both ways. In case you decide to strain your ookha you may add to it (just before serving) 2-3 tablespoons of very dry sherry wine and sprinkle the top of each serving with finely chopped fresh dill. If you serve your ookha unstrained, heap a tablespoon of sour cream over each serving and sprinkle with fresh dill. The unstrained soup is more difficult to serve. There might be some tiny bones in the soup, so be very careful in giving it to children. My wise grandmother combined both ideas. She strained the soup, but put back all the best boneless pieces of fish!

This recipe will serve four to six people.

Fish Soup Purée (Ookha Purée)

This is another way of preparing ookha.

3 pounds of 2-3 kinds of white-fleshed fish
6-7 cups water
1 carrot
1 onion
1 parsnip
1 stalk celery
5-6 peppercorns
2 bay leaves
1 tablespoon lemon juice
2 tablespoons dry sherry wine
Salt, according to taste

Bring water to a quick boil and add the sliced vegetables and spices. Simmer for 10-15 minutes. Add half of the fish and cook until the fish begins to fall apart. Strain the soup through a fine sieve, take out bay leaves and peppercorns. Force the remaining vegetables and pieces of fish through a fine sieve. Return the mass to the fish stock and bring to a boil once more. Add the remaining half of the raw and boned fish, cut into serving pieces. Cook slowly for about 10-15 minutes or until the slices of fish are tender but don't allow them to start falling apart. Just before serving add lemon juice or sherry wine. Serve with a piece of fish for each serving.

The Russians usually eat the broth first, together with little pastries filled with rice or fish or other things, keeping the boiled fish from the ookha for a second course. In such case, have some fresh horse-radish for garnish. Serves four to six people.

FRESH MUSHROOM SOUP

1/2 cup mushrooms, washed
    and sliced
2 cups water
2 cups milk (or 4 cups water)
3-4 tablespoons butter
1 large onion

2-3 potatoes
2 tablespoons pearl barley or
    long-grained rice
Sour cream
Salt and pepper, according
    to taste

Sauté sliced onion in butter until tender, but don't let it get brown. Add mushrooms and more butter if necessary and continue to sauté for another 5-6 minutes. Combine barley (or rice) with salt, pepper and water (using all 4 cups if you don't intend to use milk), boil for 40-45 minutes or until the grain is just about done. Add potatoes and continue to cook until all ingredients are tender. Add milk and bring to a quick boil. Serve with a heaping spoonful of sour cream for each serving. If the soup looks too thick, add more water or milk, stirring it in thoroughly. Serves four to six.

FRUIT SOUP (MALINNICK)

3 1/2 cups hulled raspberries
3 1/2 cups water
3/4 cup red dessert wine (or
    Rose)

3/4 cup sugar (or more)
1/2 teaspoon vanilla extract
3/4 cup heavy sour cream
Dash of salt

Select only the ripest berries. Force them through a fine sieve. Combine sugar with sour cream and beat it slightly with an egg-beater. Add vanilla and salt. Add water very slowly, stirring the mixture all the time, then add wine. Combine with the berries.

Heat the mixture on a very slow fire, stirring it all the time. Do not allow to boil.

You may serve this soup either hot or cold. The hot soup does wonders for a sore throat, while the cold one tastes almost like dessert. Use a few extra-handsome berries as a garnish for both versions.

You may experiment with almost any kind of fresh berries in making this soup. Pitted cherries are excellent, as are strawberries, red or black currants, or boysenberries. Or you may use several kinds of berries in one soup. Vary the amount of sugar to taste, for some berries are sweeter than others.

Serves four to six people.

APPLE SOUP, SERVED COLD (YABLONNICK)

This refreshing, delicious, cold sweet soup, made of apples, has always been a favorite of children.

5-6 large tart apples, cored	*1 cup sugar*
and skinned	*1 teaspoon vanilla extract*
4 cups water	*3-4 whole cloves*

Combine diced apples and sugar and let them stand for a few minutes, while you boil the water.

Put sugared apples and cloves into rapidly boiling water and reduce heat at once. Simmer slowly until the apples are completely soft.

Add vanilla and remove from fire.

Cool thoroughly before serving. Serve with thin vanilla wafers or hard Holland rusk.

Serves four to six people.

FISH SOLYANKA

This is a very thick fish soup and it is so nourishing that seldom would you want to eat anything else after it but dessert and coffee. It is a typical Russian one-course meal—and a delicious one!

1 1/4 pounds any fish for making fish stock
3/4 pound fresh salmon fillet
3 1/2 or 4 cups water
2-3 potatoes, sliced with a fancy cutter
1-2 carrots, sliced with a fancy cutter
2 small tomatoes, skinned and quartered
4-5 dill pickles

1-2 onions
1 bay leaf
1 tablespoon green and black olives, chopped
1 teaspoon capers' juice
1 tablespoon capers
3-4 tablespoons butter
6 peppercorns
Salt and pepper, according to taste
1 lemon, thinly sliced

Wash and clean but do not skin or bone the fish. Combine with water, bay leaf, peppercorns and salt, and make a fish stock. Chop onions, pickles and olives. Cut potatoes and carrots with a fancy cutter, making some attractive cut-outs.

Strain the fish stock. Put into it cut potatoes and carrots and cook until the vegetables are just about tender. Cut salmon into serving pieces and place them in the pot together with diced onions, pickles, olives, capers, capers' juice and butter. Cover with a lid and cook for 5 minutes. Remove the lid and cook for another 5-10 minutes without the lid.

Slice lemon very thinly, removing the rind. Serve hot, with a slice of lemon over each serving and a dash of freshly chopped dill or parsley. You may add to solyanka the meat of boiled fish from which the basic stock was made, but be sure to remove all the bones.

Serves four to six people.

FISH

A country of many seas and rivers, of two oceans—Pacific and Arctic—Russia is the country of a great variety of fish and it is only natural that Russians just love fish! They serve it in countless ways—boiled, smoked, fried, dried, marinated, salted, under mayonnaise, in aspic and many other ways, like steamed or grated.

Here are a few Russian hints about preparing fish:

1. Always have enough butter (or margarine) while frying fish. If you don't have enough butter while you're frying, and have to add it during the process, the fish won't fry evenly and might get burned.

2. Fish always has to be cooked completely.

3. If you're boiling very fresh fish, don't add any spices. The taste of the very fresh fish is better than any spices.

4. If you're cooking just-caught fish, make a slash along its back to prevent tearing of the skin during the process of cooking.

5. To avoid confusion, we have two different words: *marinade,* a noun and *marinate,* a verb.

Marinade is a spicy sauce which we serve with the fish (and sometimes with meat) and which is usually served cold. But when we want to marinate fish or meat we usually leave the product to be marinated in some special marinade and let it marinate for several hours. Confusing, isn't it?

HERRING

1 large herring
2 cucumbers
1 1/4 pounds cooked whole
      potatoes

1/4 pound unsalted butter
1 tablespoon chopped parsley
  or dill

Prepare a large herring by soaking its fillets in milk for one or two hours. Press fillets one against the other and cut the herring into one-inch-thick slices.

Decorate the sides of the herring with round slices of cucumbers and sprinkle the top with chopped fresh parsley or dill. Serve the hot potatoes with plenty of unsalted butter from a separate dish.

MARINATED FISH

Any fresh fish can be marinated. Russians prefer to use large ones, like sturgeon, salmon, pike, or catfish (but any others may be used). Marinated fish makes good zakoosky.

1 large fresh fish
3 tablespoons vegetable oil
Flour—enough to roll the
    pieces of fish
Salt and pepper according to
    taste
Marinade:
2-3 carrots
1 stalk of celery
2-3 onions

3-4 teaspoon vegetable oil
1 1/4 cups tomato paste (or
    purée)
2 bay leaves
3-5 whole cloves
1/2 teaspoon cinnamon
1 teaspoon sugar
2/3 cup diluted vinegar
1 1/3 cups of fish stock
Salt and pepper according to
    taste

Clean the fish thoroughly and from the bones and the well-washed head and tail, cook a fish-stock (2 cups of water, without salt).

Cut the fish into serving pieces, sprinkle with salt and pepper, roll in flour and quickly fry on both sides in vegetable oil.

When the fish is ready, put it on absorbent paper and let it cool.

Prepare the following marinade:

Cut carrots, celery, onions and brown them thoroughly in vegetable oil (about 10-15 minutes).

Add tomato paste and herbs—crumbled bay leaf, cloves, cinnamon.

Cover with a lid and simmer on a slow fire for 15-20 minutes.

Add vinegar, fish stock, and bring to a quick boil.

Add sugar, salt and pepper. Cool the marinade.

Just before serving arrange the cooled pieces of fish in a deep fish platter (or any deep dish), pour over the fish the cooled marinade and serve together with hot buttered whole potatoes, sprinkled with a little chopped parsley or chopped dill. Serves four to six.

FISH A LA MAYONNAISE

1 1/4 pounds fillet of sole or salmon or trout or any other fish, boned (save the bones for the preparation of a fish stock)
1 1/4 cups mayonnaise
1 tablespoon gelatin (for 1 cup of fish stock)

1-2 bay leaves
1 whole carrot
1 uncut stalk of celery
1 dill pickle
Salt and pepper according to taste

Prepare the fish stock from the bones, head and caviar of the fish, together with carrot, celery and bay leaves. Cool the stock, take out the carrot, celery and the bay leaves, saving the carrot and celery for decoration. Strain the stock through a fine cheesecloth. Cut fillet of fish into serving pieces, sprinkle with salt and pepper. Grease a pan or a shallow pot with vegetable oil and put the fish into it, adding enough water to half cover the fish. Cover with a lid and cook slowly until the fish is soft (but do not allow it to overcook and fall apart).

When the fish is ready, put it into a serving platter and allow to cool. Meanwhile, prepare the following mayonnaise:

Dissolve gelatin in 1 cup of cooled fish stock. Mix thoroughly with mayonnaise. Cover each piece of the fish with the mayonnaise sauce and decorate the tops with slices of cooked carrot and celery, together with round slices of dill pickle.

To make an even more attractive dish, decorate the tops

of fish pieces with slices of hard-boiled egg, pouring the mayonnaise mixture thinly over them.

You may serve this dish with this sauce, served on the side:

2 *hard-boiled eggs, finely* *chopped*
1/4 *pound unsalted butter*
1 *tablespoon strong mustard*

1 *tablespoon chopped pars-* *ley or dill*
1/2 *teaspoon lemon juice*

Heat and melt the butter. Add chopped eggs, parsley (or dill) and mix well. Add lemon juice. Serve the sauce hot. Serves four to six.

FORSHMAK

An unusual hot dish which may be also served cold as a very tasty "left-over."

2 *large herrings*
2 *eggs, beaten*
1 *large onion, chopped very* *fine*
1 *tart apple, grated*
5-6 *cooked and mashed po-* *tatoes*

1-2 *slices of stale white* *bread, without crust*
2 *tablespoons bread crumbs*
Salt and pepper according to *taste (not TOO much salt!)*

Remove all the bones from the herrings and soak them in milk for two or three hours. In a separate dish, soak bread in a small amount of milk. Meanwhile, brown the chopped onion in a small amount of unsalted butter.

Grate the apple and beat the eggs until very smooth but not dry. Put the drained herring and browned onion together through a fine meat grinder.

Combine the herring mixture with grated apple and place it in a greased baking dish.

Add the soaked bread (with the excess of milk squeezed out) to the egg mixture and spread it on top of herring.

Cover the very top of the dish with mashed potatoes, squeezing them through a pastry tube in order to make some attractive designs (or simply heap the potatoes over) and bake in a moderate oven (350°) for 25-30 minutes.

Five minutes before the forshmak is ready, sprinkle the top with bread crumbs and let them turn golden. Serves four to six.

SHASHLIK OF SALMON

Particularly suitable for informal buffet dinners or at barbecue parties.

1 pound fillet of fresh salmon
1 pound mushrooms (use only caps)
1 tablespoon lemon juice
Bread crumbs

1/2 pint sour cream
1/4 pound red caviar
Salt and pepper, according to taste

Clean, bone, and wash fillet of salmon and immediately wipe it dry. Cut into thick chunks (about 2 inches square). Season slightly with salt and pepper (go easy on salt) and sprinkle with lemon juice (or rub each chunk generously with a wedge of lemon). Sauté mushrooms (caps only) in butter. Roll salmon chunks in bread crumbs and place them on skewers, alternating with mushroom caps.

Grill over (or under) a medium flame in your broiler (it takes longer to do it over an open grill).

Mix sour cream with red caviar, trying not to break the individual beads of caviar.

Serve very hot, with hot boiled potatoes and caviar mixture on the side. If this is for a barbecue, have mushrooms sautéed ahead of time. Have all the ingredients ready and handy and let the guests make their own shashliks.

FLOUNDER A LA GREQUE (SUDAK PO GRECHESKI)

3 pounds fillet of flounder
3 cups water
3 tablespoons butter
1 large onion, chopped very
  fine
3-4 ripe tomatoes
1/2 pound fresh spinach
1/2 sorrel (sour grass)
2-3 scallions

2-3 stalks parsley, chopped
2 dill pickles, chopped
1 tablespoon dill pickle juice
1 clove garlic
Salt and pepper, according
  to taste
Lemon slices, with rind re-
  moved

Chop onions and garlic. Peel tomatoes, cut them in 8 parts each. Chop spinach, sorrel and scallions. Brown onions and garlic in butter and combine with the rest of the vegetables. Sauté until tender. Add chopped parsley and pickles and pickle juice. Add hot water. Bring to a boil. Add seasoning.

Cut fillet of flounder into serviceable pieces and place them on top of vegetables. Cover with lid and cook for about 10 minutes. Prepare a deep hot platter to receive fish. Take the fish out of the cooking pot and place it on the platter, heaping each piece with the cooked vegetables and fish stock.

If the stock appears to look like soup, being too thin, drain the vegetables, add to the stock 1-2 tablespoon of flour mixed with cold water and bring the stock to a quick boil. The stock should have the appearance of a thin gravy.

Serve at once, with thin slices of lemon to top each serving. As a side vegetable, serve boiled buttered potatoes.

Serves four to six people.

PERCH WITH SOUR CREAM (OKOON V SMETANE)

6-7 small perch (or any small, white-meat fish)
1 cup sour cream
1/2 cup fish stock
1 onion, chopped
1 bunch parsley, chopped fine

4 tablespoons flour
Butter
Salt and pepper according to taste

Clean and cut fish into serving pieces. Roll in flour and fry in butter on both sides. Put fish into a baking dish and pour over it the following sauce:

Cut and sauté one onion in butter. Transfer the prepared onion into the pan in which the fish was fried. Add fish stock and sour cream. Dissolve flour in a small amount of water and add to the sour-cream mixture. Boil quickly, letting the sauce thicken. Pour the sauce over the fish and bake in a hot oven for 10-15 minutes.

Chop parsley very fine and sprinkle it generously over the fish just before serving. Serve at once with hot boiled potatoes as a side dish.

You may also add hard-boiled eggs to your sauce. Chop two hard-boiled (and cooled) eggs and sprinkle them over the fish and sauce before putting the fish into the oven. Bake for only 10 minutes and watch all the time that the eggs don't become too dry. Add a pat of butter if necessary.

Serves four to six people.

FLOUNDER WITH MUSHROOM SAUCE

3 pounds flounder
1 pound mushrooms
1 cup sour cream
1 1/2 tablespoons flour
2-3 bay leaves
6 peppercorns

1/2 cup (or more) vinegar
Soup greens
2 cups of water
Salt and pepper according to
*   taste*

Clean flounder and cut it in serving pieces. Pour vinegar over the fish and let it stand under cover for one hour.

Meanwhile, cook soup greens, bay leaves, and peppercorns in two cups of water for 1/2 hour. Add fish and simmer until fish is tender.

Prepare the following sauce:

Wash and cut mushrooms and sauté them in butter until slightly brown. Cover with just enough water and simmer until tender. Dissolve flour in a small amount of water and add to the mushrooms together with sour cream. Bring to a very quick boil and serve right away, pouring the sauce over the fish.

Serve with hot boiled potatoes on the side.

Serves four to six people.

MEAT

Russians have an endless variety of recipes for meat dishes, all famous and approved by restaurants and celebrities. I won't even try to introduce anything new. I'll just try to concentrate on some good, proven, famous dishes, which make any Russian's mouth water and which, I hope, will do the same for you.

Here are a few secrets which may be helpful in cooking meats:

1. To have a chunk of meat fried or broiled evenly, pound it slightly with a meat mallet before cooking. This also helps to tenderize tougher cuts of meat.

2. Whenever you cook any kind of meat on the top of the stove, start with a hot temperature, to let the meat close its pores, and thus preserve the juice. Then reduce the heat and finish cooking at more moderate temperature.

3. Don't dispose of any tough parts of meat (or bones). Instead, wash them and, while you prepare your dinner, let the bones and the tough parts simmer slowly. This way, you'll always have some wonderful, home-made meat stock, needed in preparing so many main dishes. Of course, you can always use ready-made canned consommé in place of the home-made stock, but if you are like me you prefer the home-made ingredients. Especially, since it doesn't require any additional work—just watch that it doesn't boil over!

4. If you are making a soup, using meat or fish, and if you don't intend to serve boiled meat or fish as the main course, put the meat or fish through a grinder, add necessary seasoning and sautéed onions or mushrooms, and use the mass for stuffing pirozhky or pirogy.

5. If you have a few kotlety left, use them the next day served in a casserole, under your favorite sauce. Or you may slice the kotlety lengthwise, sprinkle with salt and serve cold, between two slices of buttered bread, as a sandwich.

6. Sometimes you may use a few remaining kotlety as a stuffing for fried kabatchky or baclazhany (stuffed squash or stuffed egg plant). In such case, the kotlety must be put through a meat grinder while cold, then slightly browned in butter and used as a stuffing, following the procedure mentioned in the particular recipe.

7. Any kind of roolet is good either hot or cold. Serve it sliced in a sandwich, or reheat it in the oven, watching that it doesn't become too dry (cover it with a thick fold of waxed paper). Serve reheated roolet under any of the suitable sauces—tomato, mushroom, egg or sour cream.

8. Any meat dish cooked in wine may be reheated. Add

a little of the same wine before serving, to restore the aroma.

9. When making beef à la Stroganoff, never allow sour cream to cook for a long time. It loses its flavor and curdles, releasing a lot of butter fat. Always add sour cream during the last phase of your cooking—unless the recipe advises otherwise.

10. Be careful in cooking liver. Only 2-3 minutes of extra cooking time might spoil the taste of liver and make it dry and tough.

11. When broiling beef, never season it until it is just about to be served. The reason for this rule is that salt melts and makes the raw meat too wet, and pepper burns under the broiler, loses its aroma and gives the meat a bitter taste.

12. To marinate meat in a short time (about 30-40 minutes), cut the meat into serving pieces and pound them with a meat mallet. Add 2 chopped onions, bay leaf, 3 tablespoons olive oil, juice of 1/4 lemon and 1/2 teaspoon salt. Stir the meat often to let the marinade penetrate each piece.

PÂTÉ (PASHTET) OF LIVER

Pashtet of liver has been one of my favorite dishes ever since my childhood. My grandmother used to prepare me days ahead for the occasion of having pashtet for dinner. I had to be a good girl for at least two weeks before the great day, minding my manners at the table, not interrupting the grown-ups when they talked, not talking unless talked to! It was a hard thing to do—but the reward was worth it. Here is my grandmother's recipe for this tasty and good-looking dish.

2 pounds fresh baby-beef   2-3 sprigs of celery tops
  liver   1-2 sprigs of parsley tops
1 large carrot   3 slices of stale white bread
2 medium-sized onions   2 eggs
1 bay leaf   Salt and pepper according to
4-5 strips of bacon   taste

Boil liver, carrot, onions, celery, parsley and bay leaf in a small amount of water until tender. Take out the bay leaf, carrot, celery and parsley. Broil the bacon slices until slightly golden (but do not overbroil!). Drain the liver (save the stock). Grind liver, onion, and bacon through a meat grinder. Add salt and pepper according to your taste.

Soak in water slightly stale white bread (without crust), squeeze water out and add to the liver mixture.

Beat two eggs and work them into the liver mixture too. If the mixture looks too coarse—work it through a sieve or cream it with a wooden spatula until very creamy. Add gradually 1 1/2 cups of strained liver stock. Put into a well-greased baking dish and bake for 20-30 minutes in a moderate oven (350°). Cool and decorate the top, if you wish, with slices of hard-boiled eggs or slices of black and green olives or green onions, chopped very fine.

Serve cold as a main dish with hot buttered potatoes or it may be served as an appetizer. It keeps its taste for a long time if stored in the refrigerator in a glass dish. Pashtet makes a very attractive party dish for buffet style informal dinners. Serves four to six.

MOSKOVSKAYA SOLYANKA

Here is a dish which in Russia is the equivalent of an American tossed salad—anything can be put into it!

But, unlike a salad, solyanka is served hot and in a casserole. For those who crave sauerkraut, this is a must!

1 1/2 pounds sauerkraut, drained (save the sauerkraut stock)
2 smoky links (sausage)
3 frankfurters
3-4 slices bologna
1-2 slices ham
4 tablespoons butter
1 cup sauerkraut stock (or less)

1 large onion, chopped
2/3 cup mushrooms, chopped
1/4 cup black olives, chopped
1 bay leaf
1 tablespoon flour
Salt and pepper according to taste

Sauté onion in butter until golden. In a separate pan sauté mushrooms until soft. Combine onions and mushrooms, sprinkle with flour and sauté together for another minute or two.

Add sauerkraut and sliced frankfurters, ham, bologna and olives. Add salt and pepper, sauerkraut stock and serve hot.

This is a meal in itself and it is a wonderful and exotic way to get rid of a lot of left-over cold cuts. Serves six.

BEEF A LA STROGANOFF I

One of the best-known Russian main dishes in America is, of course, Beef à la Stroganoff. There are several ways to prepare this delectible dish.

Each of my Russian friends in America insists that his or her recipe for Beef Stroganoff is the only authentic one.

The real purists would never add mushrooms nor tomato paste to their recipe. Personally, I like to have mushrooms in my Beef Stroganoff, but in all fairness, I shall give alternative ideas on how to make this tasty dish, which is so convenient to serve as a hot entrée at informal buffet-style dinners.

1 1/2 pounds tenderloin of beef	*1 small onion*
1/2 cup sour cream	*1/2 pound mushrooms, sliced*
1 cup stock or water	*Salt and pepper, according to taste*
2 tablespoons whole-wheat flour	*1 strip of dry crust from a slice of pumpernickel bread*
2-3 tablespoons butter	

Cut beef into shoestring strips and roll each strip in flour. Brown meat quickly on all sides, putting only a few pieces at a time on your frying pan. In separate pans, sauté onions and mushrooms. Combine with meat, add stock or water and the strip of pumpernickel crust. Add salt and pepper. Simmer until the meat is tender. Add sour cream and bring to a quick boil.

Don't allow the mixture at any time to get stuck to the bottom of your pan. Add some more stock or hot water if necessary, one tablespoon at a time. Serve hot, together with hot boiled potatoes, sprinkled with chopped dill or parsley. Beef Stroganoff also goes well with noodles. Serves four to six persons.

BEEF A LA STROGANOFF II

1 1/2 pounds tenderloin of beef	*2 tablespoons tomato paste*
1/2 pound mushrooms	*2-3 tablespoons flour*
1/2 cup sour cream	*2-3 tablespoons butter*
1 cup beef stock or water	*Salt and pepper according to taste*
2 onions, chopped	

Cut beef into small chunks and roll each chunk in flour. Fry quickly in butter. Add salt and pepper.

Sauté onions in butter. Add tomato paste. Stir in one tablespoon of flour and slowly add beef stock or water. Simmer the mixture, stirring all the time. When mixture thickens, add cut mushrooms and continue to simmer for another 10-15 minutes. Combine beef pieces with the mushroom mixture and add sour cream. Bring to a quick boil. Serve with boiled rice. Serves four to six people.

BEEF A LA STROGANOFF III

This recipe calls for mustard and must be made in a double-boiler.

1 1/2 pounds tenderloin of beef	2-3 tablespoons butter
	2-3 tablespoons flour
1 cup beef consommé or water	1 teaspoon mustard, preferably hot
1/2 cup sour cream	Salt and pepper, according to taste
1 onion, sliced into large slices	

Cut meat into shoestring strips. Sprinkle with salt and pepper and let it stand at room temperature for one hour.

Meanwhile, dissolve 2 tablespoons of flour in a small amount of consommé or water and mix with the remaining amount of consommé or water. Dissolve mustard in this and bring it to a quick boil. Add sour cream.

Dust the remaining flour over the strips of meat and fry each strip on all sides in butter, together with onions. Take the onions out and combine meat only with the mustard sauce. Cover with a lid and cook in a double-boiler for 20-30 minutes, stirring quite often.

As soon as the meat is tender, serve at once, together with hot boiled potatoes or boiled rice. Serves four to six.

To an American, who is accustomed to mushrooms or onions or tomato paste in his Beef à la Stroganoff, this recipe might appear strange. But try it, nevertheless, try it the real Russian way, and I'm sure you'll like it too! Besides, this, mushroomless and onionless, is a wonderful "streamlined" recipe for those days when you don't have too many ingredients at your finger tips!

KOTLETY

Kotlety—small ground-meat patties—are a cross between an American hamburger and a Swedish meat ball. There are several varieties of kotlety, each under its own name, each having (or omitting) some particular ingredients, but all of them basically the same—meat patties.

Just as there are many ways to prepare kotlety, there are equally many ways to prepare the sauce, *podlivka*, for them. I'll give here several ideas, but let your imagination carry you and you'll be able to create your own podlivka's.

BASIC KOTLETY

1 1/2 pounds ground beef chuck	1/2 teaspoon pepper
1 onion	1 egg
2-3 slices of stale white bread, without crust	4-5 tablespoons butter
3/4 teaspoon salt	2 tablespoons sour cream
	Bread crumbs or corn meal

Soak stale bread in a small amount of cold milk or water. Squeeze the liquid out.

Put the meat through a meat grinder. Add stale bread and

put the mass through the grinder again. Grate the onion, mix with meat and add salt and pepper. Beat the egg very lightly and add to the meat mixture, stirring with a wooden spoon until everything is completely smooth. Have the frying pan evenly hot (but not overhot). Melt the butter. Keep butter hot while you are shaping the kotlety from the meat mixture. Make small oval or round patties, somewhat smaller than the usual size of an American hamburger. Roll them quickly in bread crumbs or corn meal and flatten them with a knife, criss-crossing their flat sides with a knife.

Brown kotlety in butter for 5 minutes on each side. Do not overcrowd your frying pan—you'll break the kotlety while turning them over if there are too many of them in your pan at the same time. As kotlety become done, put them on a hot platter. Put a little more butter into your frying pan and 2-3 tablespoons of water. Bring to a quick boil, stirring all the time with a fork. Add 2 tablespoons sour cream. Pour the sauce over the kotlety and serve at once. Serves four to six people.

POZHARSKY KOTLETY

1 pound cooked veal or meat from one stewing chicken (or 1/2 pound veal and the white meat from one stewing chicken)	*1/4 pound butter*
	1 tablespoon melted butter
	2 eggs
	1 1/2 cups consommé
	Bread crumbs
6 stale slices of white bread, without the crust	*Milk*
	Salt and pepper, according to taste
1 small onion, chopped very fine	

Soak stale bread in a small amount of milk. Squeeze dry. Put meat through a meat grinder and combine with bread.

Fry chopped onion in 1 tablespoon of butter until golden and add to meat. Season to your taste. Beat one egg very slightly and add to the meat mixture. Thoroughly mix and form into plump oval cutlets. Beat another egg with 1-2 tablespoons of water. Dip each cutlet into the egg and roll in bread crumbs.

Have the frying pan evenly hot (but not burning). Fry the cutlets in 1/4 pound of butter for 5 minutes on each side. Remove from the pan and put into warm casserole dish (keep it warm over a pan of hot water).

Prepare the following sauce:

1 cup fresh or canned sliced mushrooms
2 tablespoons butter
1 tablespoon flour
1/2 teaspoon coarse pepper
1 teaspoon lemon juice

Sauté mushrooms in butter for 5 minutes. Sprinkle with pepper. Dissolve flour in 1/2 cup of cold consommé and pour over the mushrooms. Add lemon juice. Cover with a lid and simmer for 10 minutes. Meanwhile, pour 1 cup of remaining consommé into the pan where you fried your pozharsky kotlety, simmer, stirring with a fork. Add mushroom sauce to the consommé in the frying pan, mix thoroughly, and bring to a quick boil.

Pour the sauce over the pozharsky kotlety in the casserole dish and serve at once. As a side dish, Russians usually serve mashed potatoes or noodles. Serves four to six people.

RUSSIAN MEAT LOAF WITH RICE—ZRAZY

Like people the world over, Russians love all kinds of meat loaves, which are so economical to prepare and so nourishing to eat. The recipe which follows some people call Polish Zrazy but—Polish or Russian—zrazy is a very tasty dish, delicious when served hot and equally good when served cold, looking quite attractive in both versions.

1 1/2 pounds round steak	*2 tablespoons flour*
1/2 pound pork or sugar-cured ham	*Butter*
Capers
3 onions, sliced	*2 bay leaves*
1/2 cup mushrooms, sliced	*Salt and pepper, according to taste*
1 cup cooked rice	
2 cups sour cream	

Put round steak and pork (or ham) through a coarse meat grinder. Season with salt and pepper and fry slightly in butter, stirring with a fork. In another pan, brown onions and mushrooms in butter, add capers and mix well. Grease a baking dish and place in it a layer of meat, then a layer of cooked rice, then a layer of mushrooms and onions, then the remaining rice and finally, a layer of meat again.

Make the following sauce:

Mix flour and sour cream in the pan, where the meat was fried, adding a little butter if necessary. Add the bay leaves and pour the sauce over the meat loaf. Bake in a moderate oven (350°) for 30-40 minutes or until tender. Serve with cooked red cabbage or mashed potatoes. Serves four to six people.

KIDNEY IN MADEIRA WINE

2 baby-beef or veal kidneys	*Flour*
2 tablespoons butter	*Salt and pepper according to taste*
1/2 cup Madeira wine	
1 tablespoon sour cream	

Remove all fat, skin and gristle from the kidneys and slice them very thin. Sprinkle the kidneys with flour and shake vigorously. Sauté in hot butter very small amounts of sliced kidneys (not more than 2-3 tablespoons at a time, so that the pieces won't stick together). Each batch has to be sautéed for not more than 3-4 minutes. Put the kidneys into a serving dish.

In the pan where you've fried the kidneys, put sour cream, wine and seasoning and bring to a quick boil. Pour the sauce over the kidneys and serve at once. As a side dish, serve small new potatoes or new green peas or French cut beans. Serves four to six people.

BAKED KOTLETY

1 1/2 pounds ground beef
1/2 pound ground pork (or fresh sausage)
3 slices of stale white bread, without crust
1 cup consommé or water
3-4 tablespoons butter
2 eggs
1 teaspoon dill or parsley, minced fine
1 tablespoon scallion, minced fine
3-4 tablespoon sour cream
1 teaspoon salt
1/2 teaspoon pepper
Flour
Milk

Put the beef and pork through your meat grinder. Add salt and pepper. Soak bread in a small amount of milk and squeeze dry. Add to the meat together with minced dill or parsley and scallion. Mix very thoroughly. Add egg yolks and continue to mix. Whip the egg whites until stiff and add to the mixture.

Shape kotlety into small oval or round patties and fry in the preheated pan for 5 minutes on each side. Place the fried kotlety in a warm baking dish and prepare the following sauce:

Sprinkle a little flour into the frying pan in which you have just fried the kotlety. Brown the flour and add consommé or water and sour cream. Stir constantly and bring to a quick boil.

Pour the sauce over the kotlety, cover with a lid and bake for 20-25 minutes in a moderate oven (350°).

Serve at once with hot boiled potatoes or noodles.

Serves four to six people.

SAUCE—PODLIVKA FOR KOTLETY

The easiest and the fastest podlivka is made from the pan-thickened gravy.

Sprinkle a little flour into the pan where you fried your kotlety. Let it brown, stirring constantly with a fork. Then, add one cup of consommé or water and any of the following ingredients:

1. Sour cream
2. Tomato paste or ketchup
3. Chili sauce
4. Mustard
5. Chopped and sautéed onions
6. Sliced and sautéed mushrooms
7. Chopped hard-boiled egg
8. Chopped and sautéed green onions
9. Chopped fried bacon and capers . . . and many other things you might think about. The amount of these ingredients depends on how many of them you happen to have or happen to like—in other words, it is entirely up to you. So,

here is your chance to create something new, for any cook with creative ability can improve any tried and proven recipe.

THREE-TIERED MEAT LOAF

Looks very attractive when it is sliced into uniform portions. It is made of three kinds of meat and tastes very good either hot or cold.

1 pound ground round steak
1 pound ground pork (or 1 pound cooked ground liver)
1 pound ground veal
3-4 slices bacon
3-4 slices of stale white bread, without crust
1 large onion, chopped very fine
1/2 cup sour cream
2 eggs
1 cup finely chopped green onions or scallions
2 tablespoons finely chopped parsley
1-2 tablespoons butter
1 tablespoon flour
Sifted bread crumbs
Milk
Dash of nutmeg
Salt and pepper, according to taste

Soak bread in milk and squeeze it dry. Put through a meat-grinder each kind of meat separately, adding equal amounts of soaked bread and seasoning to each of the meats. Keep the ground meats in separate containers until ready to use.

Sauté chopped onion and, in another pan, sauté the chopped green onions or scallions. Keep them separated also.

Cream eggs with 1-2 tablespoons of milk and divide the mixture between the three kinds of meat, working it into each of them with your hands. Grease a baking dish and shape the ingredients into a meat-loaf form, starting with one kind of meat, following with a layer of sautéed onions, then, the layer of another kind of meat, following with a layer of sautéed green onions or scallions and, finally, the last kind of meat. Sprinkle the loaf generously with bread crumbs and cover the top with the slices of bacon.

Bake in a hot oven (400°) for 15-20 minutes, then reduce heat to 350° and continue to bake for another 30-40 minutes. Keep basting every 10-15 minutes.

When the loaf is ready, remove into a hot platter and discard the bacon slices.

Skim the fat from the juice in the pan and sprinkle one tablespoon of flour into the pan, stirring constantly. Add a little water, sour cream, and a dash of nutmeg and bring to a quick boil.

Serve the sauce in a separate dish.

As a side dish, hot boiled or mashed potatoes are the best.

Serves four to six people.

CABBAGE LEAVES STUFFED WITH MEAT AND RICE (GOLUBTZI)

10-12 large cabbage leaves
1 pound ground round steak
1/2 pound ground pork (or 1/2 pound unseasoned pork sausage)
1 cup cooked rice
1 cup tomato juice
1 cup water
1/2 cup sour cream
2 tablespoons minced parsley
1 egg
1 large onion, chopped
4 tablespoons butter
2 tablespoons flour
Salt and pepper according to taste

Get a large, crisp head of cabbage. Select the best and the largest leaves. Cut off the hardest parts. Put the leaves into hot, salty water for 10 minutes and put them on a towel to dry, spreading them very gently, so as not to tear any of them.

Mix the ground beef and pork with rice. Sauté onions in a little butter and mix them with a raw egg. Add salt and pepper and combine thoroughly with the meat mixture. Put the stuffing into each leaf of cabbage, making very neat little packages, and tie each package with a string.

Fry in hot butter until brown on each side, cover with a lid and cook slowly for 25-30 minutes, adding a little butter if necessary.

Very carefully, remove the strings from each of the golubtzi. Take the golubtzi out of the pan and put them on a platter. Sprinkle flour into the pan where the golubtzi were fried. Cook slowly for 5 minutes, stirring constantly. Add tomato juice and water and bring to a quick boil. Add sour cream and salt and pepper. Pour the gravy over golubtzi and serve at once. Serves four to six people.

LAMB BROILED ON SKEWERS (SHISH KEBAB)

Shish kebab makes a spectacular dish for informal buffet-style dinners. It is extremely easy to prepare; even the men love to preside over its broiling.

1 leg of lamb	*1 1/2 teaspoons salt*
2 large onions, sliced	*1/2 teaspoon coarse pepper*
1 cup mushroom caps, whole	*1 teaspoon oregano*
2 tablespoons olive oil	*Tomatoes*
3 tablespoons dry sherry wine	

Bone the leg of lamb, remove all fat and gristle. Save the best pieces of fat for later use. Cut the meat into 1 1/2 inch chunks. Combine all the ingredients together and put them into a large pan or mixing bowl, cover and let it marinate for several hours. I usually prepare the ingredients the night before I intend to use them, for the longer the lamb marinates, the better it will taste.

Plan your meal in such a way that you can serve your shish kebab right from the broiler (or barbecue pit). Have enough skewers to accommodate each guest, for it is more attractive to serve shish kebab directly from the skewers.

String the chunks of lamb on the skewers, alternating them with the mushroom caps or thick slices of firm tomatoes (or, even whole tomatoes if they are of small Italian variety), and thick, round slices of onion.

Put little chunks of lamb's fat on the skewers here and there. Broil in the oven broiler or, better, over a charcoal fire.

Turn the skewers as necessary to assure an even crispness on all sides. When the meat is sufficiently done—and you'll have to decide yourself how well done you want it—serve it at once.

For a side dish serve rice pilaff.

RICE PILAFF

3 cups rice
6 cups beef or chicken stock (or canned chicken or beef consommé)
1 medium-sized onion (optional)

3 tablespoons butter
Salt and pepper, according to taste

Melt butter and add dry rice. (Most rice sold in America is so clean that it is not necessary to wash it. However, if you wash your rice, make sure that it is absolutely dry before you follow this recipe.) Braise the rice slowly, stirring it constantly, until the butter begins to hiss and to bubble.

Sauté the onion in a separate pan until golden and combine with rice.

Add hot beef stock and seasoning (if you use canned consommé, which has been already seasoned, go easy on salt).

Combine the ingredients very thoroughly and place in a baking dish. Bake in a moderate oven (375°) for 25-30 minutes. Remove from the oven, stir thoroughly, sprinkle with a little melted butter and return to the oven for another 10-15 minutes.

SHASHLIK

Shashlik is very similar to the shish kebab. I suspect that even the Russians hardly know the difference. Both are made of lamb, both are broiled on skewers and both are marinated before being broiled. There is a slight difference in the ingredients of the marinade but any clever cook differs her (or his) ingredients anyway. So, let's not be pedantic and let's enjoy one more of the traditional dishes of Russian Caucasus.

1 leg of lamb	*1 small clove of garlic*
1 onion	*Coarsely ground pepper*
4 tablespoons olive oil	*Salt, according to taste*
2 tablespoons lemon juice	

Bone a leg of lamb, remove all the tendons and gristle. Cut meat into uniform chunks of about 1 1/2 inch cubes. In a large bowl, mix oil and lemon juice. Add sliced onion, garlic, salt and pepper. Add meat. Mix thoroughly, making sure that each piece of meat is covered with oil and lemon-juice mixture. Cover with a lid and place in a refrigerator overnight.

When about ready to serve, string the chunks of lamb on skewers, alternating them with thick slices of firm tomatoes and thick, round slices of onion. Broil under an open fire in your broiler or over the charcoal fire. Turn the skewers as necessary to assure even brownness and crispness.

Serve at once with rice pilaff or with wild rice, or with Prune Pilaff.

1/2 pound prunes   *2 tablespoons butter*
1 cup pre-cooked rice

Stew the prunes and drain them. Cool. Take the pits out. Prepare the rice according to directions given on the package. Combine with prunes and mix thoroughly. Grease a baking dish and put in the rice and prune mixture. Pour over it the melted butter. Bake in a moderate oven for 10-15 minutes, or until the top turns golden.

You may add to the rice 1/4 cup of seedless raisins or substitute apricots for prunes. Or improvise to your heart's content with all kinds of dried fruits.

Serves four to six people. For more people, double or triple the recipe.

FILLET OF LAMB WITH KIDNEYS (SHASHLIK A LA KARSKY)

Shashlik à la Karsky differs from an ordinary shashlik not only because it is broiled with lamb kidneys, but also because it is served with a sauce and is broiled in rather large chunks of meat, big enough for individual portions instead of small pieces.

3 1/2 pounds fillet of lamb   *Juice of 1 lemon*
6 lamb kidneys   *1 lemon, sliced*
3 medium-sized onions   *Leaves of 1 stalk of celery*
1 bunch green onions   *Coarsely ground pepper*
3 tablespoons vinegar   *Salt, according to taste*

Cut fillet of lamb into serving portions. Remove all tendons and gristle.

Make small cuts along the sides of each piece of lamb to prevent shrinking. Cut the kidneys lengthwise and wash thoroughly.

Chop the onions and the leaves of the celery. Put the meat and the kidneys into a deep bowl and combine with the chopped onions and celery leaves. Season with salt and pepper. Pour vinegar and lemon juice over the meat. Cover with a lid and let stand for several hours (not less than 3 hours). When ready to broil, string each piece of meat on a skewer in between two pieces of kidneys. Broil under a broiler or, even better, over a charcoal fire. Make sure that the flame never touches the meat. Turn the skewers from time to time to allow the meat to brown evenly. When shashlik is ready, remove from the skewers and serve at once together with kidneys. Cut a lemon very thin and put one slice of lemon on each portion of shashlik. Mince the green onions and sprinkle them around the lemon slice (the green onions may be omitted).

Prepare the following sauce:

3 cups meat stock or canned   *3 small onions, sliced*
  consommé   *3 stalks of celery, sliced*
6 tablespoons flour   *6 tablespoons dry wine (Ma-*
6 tablespoons tomato purée   *deira or Port)*
6 tablespoons butter   *Salt and pepper, according*
3 carrots, sliced   *to taste*

Melt butter in a heavy skillet. Add flour and, stirring constantly, fry it until dark brown. Add meat stock or consommé and mix thoroughly. Add tomato purée and blend until completely mixed.

In a separate pan, brown all the vegetables slightly— onions, carrots and celery. Mix with the flour mixture and cook slowly for 20-30 minutes. At the end of cooking, add salt and pepper and wine. Strain through a fine sieve and bring to a quick boil once more.

Serve the sauce from a sauce boat.

Shashlik and sauce serve four to six people.

As a side dish serve any of the pilaff's or plain boiled rice.

MARINATED FILLETS OF BEEF ON SKEWERS (BASTROOMA)

Try this recipe for fillets of beef. It is true that there is nothing better than a real fillet and some people consider it sacrilegious to do anything but broil a good fillet. But be an adventurous soul and try Bastrooma!

3 1/2 pounds beef fillets	*3-4 tomatoes, sliced*
4 small onions	*1 lemon, sliced*
4 tablespoons fruit vinegar	*Salt and pepper according to*
1 bunch green onions	*taste*

Wash and cut off all the tendons and gristle from the fillet of beef. Cut the meat into serving pieces and put into a large china or enameled bowl.

Chop onions and add to the meat. Add vinegar and mix thoroughly. Cover with a lid and let stand in the refrigerator for 2-3 hours.

When ready to broil, string the pieces of meat on skewers

and broil over a charcoal fire or under a broiler. Do not allow the flames to touch the meat directly. Broil the bastrooma for 8-10 minutes, turning the skewers so that meat will broil evenly.

Chop the green onions and when bastrooma is ready, sprinkle each portion with green onions and decorate with thin slices or wedges of lemon. Serve at once with the sauce described in the preceding recipe (shashlik à la Karcky's sauce).

As a side dish, serve new boiled potatoes or new green peas. Serves four to six.

BAKED LAMB STEW (CHANAKHI)

2 1/2 pounds lamb stew meat (or meat from any portion of lamb)
3 pounds potatoes
1 pound tomatoes
1 pound fresh green beans
1 1/2 pounds eggplant
2 onions
2 tablespoons parsley, coarsely chopped
4 cups water (or more)
Salt and pepper, according to taste

Wash and cut meat into 2-2 1/2 inch pieces. Remove the skins from tomatoes by dipping them into boiling water or by holding them over a flame for a few seconds. Slice potatoes, tomatoes, green beans, onions and eggplant (removing of course the seeds of the eggplant and the skin). Put the meat and the sliced vegetables into a deep baking dish. Add salt and pepper and water. Cover with a lid and bake in a moderate oven (350°) for 1 1/2 to 2 hours or until ready.

Serve directly from the baking dish. Serves four to six people.

BAKED LAMB AND RICE

This is a good dish to prepare when you don't have the best cuts of lamb.

2 1/2 pounds lamb meat	*1 1/2 cups rice*
3 cups meat stock or canned	*Butter*
consommé	*Salt and pepper according to*
2 onions	*taste*

Remove all gristle from lamb. Cut into medium-sized chunks. Sprinkle with salt and pepper and brown quickly on all sides in a small amount of butter. Add chopped onions and continue to fry for 2-3 minutes more. Put the meat and the onions into a baking dish and add stock or consommé. You may also add 2-3 tablespoons tomato purée but this is optional. Cover with a lid and bake in a moderate oven (350°) for 50-60 minutes. Boil rice in rapidly boiling water for 10 minutes and then add the rice to the meat and mix thoroughly. Put the dish back in the oven and continue to bake for another 1/2 hour or until ready.

Serve directly from the baking dish. Serves four to six people.

LAMB WITH FRESH GREEN BEANS

Some time, when you don't have the best cuts of lamb, try this inexpensive way of making a very tasty dish with the minimum of ingredients.

2 1/2 pounds lamb or 6 sec-	*Water*
ond-grade lamb chops	*3-4 tablespoons butter*
2 pounds fresh green beans	*Salt and pepper, according*
2 onions	*to taste*

Cut the meat of lamb into serving pieces, removing all bones, gristle and tendons. If you use the chops, try to remove the bones also, but if it is too hard—leave them alone, they will come out by themselves when the meat is done.

Fry slightly on all sides in butter. Put the meat in a pan and cover with water, just enough to cover the top of the meat. Cover with a lid and cook slowly for 30-40 minutes.

Meanwhile, sauté the onions in a little butter. Wash and remove all the strings from the beans and cut them in small pieces. Add beans and onions to the meat. Add salt and pepper, and continue to cook until the meat and the beans are completely done.

Put the meat and the beans on a preheated platter, sprinkle with chopped dill or parsley and serve at once. Serves four to six people and can be re-heated next day without any loss of flavor.

LIVER IN SOUR CREAM

If you are tired of traditional ways of preparing liver—try this Russian recipe. It is especially good if you happened to buy some tough liver. Served with sour cream, the liver will be as soft and tender as the best grade of calf's liver.

2 1/2 pounds liver (any kind)　*2 tablespoons flour*
1 cup sour cream　*2 tablespoons dill or parsley,*
2 onions, chopped　　*chopped*
4 tablespoons butter　*Salt and pepper, according*
2 cups meat stock or water　*to taste*

Wash liver, dry and cut off all the tendons or gristle. Cut into thick slices. Sprinkle with salt and pepper, roll in flour and fry slightly on each side in butter. Sauté onions until golden brown and combine both in a deep pot. Add meat stock or water to the pan in which the liver was fried, stir well, then add sour cream. Stir well and add to the liver. Cover with a lid and cook slowly for 30-40 minutes. When the liver is ready, put the slices on a platter and pour the sour cream sauce over it. Sprinkle with dill. Serve with boiled or fried potatoes or macaroni or noodles. Serves four to six.

LAMB OR CALF KIDNEYS IN WINE SAUCE

The Russians, who adopted so many dishes from the French, also adopted the French ways of cooking with wine. I shall never forget how one of the leading actresses of Moscow invited me to dinner at her house.

She was the most honored lady of the Soviet stage, the widow of a great Russian playwright, and the most cele-brated hostess of Moscow.

"I'll prepare my own recipe of kidneys in wine sauce," she told me. "Try not to be late, for the food has to be served as soon as it is ready."

I was on time, for I never wanted to miss a chance to share the company of this great old lady. But when she opened the door for me there was a wide, happy smile on her face and her speech, that famous dramatic elocution of hers was somewhat blurred.

"You know my dear," she confessed taking me into her living room, "I'm afraid we won't have my famous kidneys tonight. You see, I had to use some Madeira wine to make the sauce. Well, in our store they had some perfectly lovely wine. . . . So, I bought it, brought it home and tried—oh, just a little wee bit. It was quite good, I thought, but I wasn't sure if it was the right kind of wine . . ." She giggled a little and continued, "Well, anyhow, I tried and I thought that it tasted really very good, so, probably it was not the right kind of wine. You know, not the cooking type. Well, I thought that maybe even if it was not the cooking type of wine, I still could use it, but I wanted to be sure." I was beginning to suspect what was coming.

"So, what happened?" I prompted. She laughed. "Oh, well, you see, I tried again and I think, again . . . And when I was ready to cook the kidney, would you believe it? The bottle was empty! ! ! What a fraud! They must've gypped me! But, worst of all, I've used all my liquor coupons for this month!"

"Don't worry, Olga Petrovna," I tried to reassure her, "I have some extra liquor coupons left, you're welcome to use them."

"Really?" she cried, "then, hurry up, get some Madeira wine before the stores close."

I brought the wine and I had to cook the kidneys, for my hostess felt too happy and giggly to do any work.

Needless to say, we had a wonderful time, for I tried some wine too while cooking, to make sure that it was of the right kind.

2 1/2 pounds kidneys (lamb or calf)	*4 tablespoons butter*
	2 tablespoons flour
1 pound mushrooms	*Salt and pepper according to*
2/3 cup Madeira wine	*taste*
2 cups meat stock or prepared consommé	

Clean the kidneys from all fat and skin. Cut lengthwise at first and then, slice into small pieces.

Sauté the mushrooms in 2 tablespoons of butter, add salt and pepper and combine with kidneys. Add the rest of the butter and fry quickly, stirring constantly. Sprinkle flour over the mixture, stir and fry for another 1-2 minutes, constantly stirring.

Add to the kidneys wine and meat stock or consommé and cook for 3-4 minutes more.

Serve on a pre-heated platter and sprinkle the top with some chopped dill or parsley (optional). Serve with boiled new potatoes or with new string beans. Serves four to six people.

BEEF KIDNEYS WITH ONION SAUCE

2 1/2 pounds beef kidneys	*2 tablespoons flour*
3 pounds potatoes	*8 peppercorns*
2 onions, chopped	*2 tablespoons minced dill or*
4-5 dill pickles	*parsley*
4-5 tablespoons butter	*Salt, according to taste*

Wash kidneys, cut off all fat and gristle. Put in a pan with cold water and bring to a boil. Pour the water out, rinse the kidneys in fresh cold water and put them back in the pan with just enough water to keep them submerged all the time. Cook slowly for 1 to 1 1/2 hours.

When the kidneys are done, take them out but save the stock for preparing the sauce.

Cut the kidneys into small pieces. Sauté the onions in a small amount of butter. Mix with the kidneys and sauté together for 3-5 minutes. Slice potatoes and fry them slightly in butter. Put the kidneys and potatoes in a pan, add sliced dill pickles and peppercorns.

Prepare the following sauce:

Sprinkle flour into the pan where you sautéed the kidneys and onions. Add the remaining butter and fry until the flour turns brown. Add 3 cups of kidney stock (and water if necessary) and mix thoroughly. Simmer for 8-10 minutes, strain, and pour over the kidneys. Cover with a lid and cook slowly for 25-30 minutes. Serve with a sprinkle of minced dill or parsley. Serves four to six people.

PORK KIDNEYS WITH ONION SAUCE

To prepare pork kidneys, follow the previous recipe and proportions. The only difference will be that you won't need to pre-cook the kidneys. You may fry them raw.

Also, if you like to cook with wine, you may add two tablespoons of dry cooking sherry just before the dish is ready to be served.

PORK SCHNITZEL A LA RUSSE

2 1/2 pounds fillet of pork or 6 pork chops with the rib bone removed
2 eggs
1 cup bread crumbs
1 tablespoon capers
1 lemon, sliced and without rind

Rind of 1 lemon, shredded very fine
4 tablespoons butter
Salt and pepper according to taste

Cut the pork into serving pieces, removing all gristle or bones.

Beat each piece with a meat mallet on both sides. Season with salt and pepper and dip in slightly beaten eggs. Roll in bread crumbs and fry quickly in butter on pre-heated skillet. When one side is golden, turn over and fry on the other side.

In a separate pan, melt some butter and quickly fry capers and shredded rind of lemon. Put the schnitzel on a pre-heated platter, pour over it the rind and capers sauce and cover each piece with a slice of lemon. Sprinkle the very middle of lemon slice with a little minced dill or parsley, but this is optional.

Serve as a side dish, fried potatoes or boiled cauliflower and your favorite green salad. Serves four to six people.

BREADED PORK CHOPS (PORK OTBIVNIE KOTLETY)

Russians always prefer to beat pork chops before frying them. They have their pork chops cut very thick and thus, after they beat the chops with a meat mallet, the pieces become not too thick, but rather large. But Russians are used to larger meals than Americans, so you don't have to order any especially thick pork chops—just a little bit thicker than your usual pork chop!

6 thick loin pork chops	*2 tablespoons minced dill or*
1 cup bread crumbs	*parsley*
2 eggs, slightly beaten	*Salt and pepper, according*
4 tablespoons butter	*to taste*

Beat each pork chop with a meat mallet on both sides. With a sharp knife, cut the meat along the bone 2/3 to the end of the bone, so that meat still will be attached to the bone. Season with salt and pepper and dip in eggs. Roll in bread crumbs very thoroughly and fry on both sides in butter on a pre-heated skillet.

When the otbivnie kotleti are ready, put them on a pre-heated platter, pour over them melted butter and meat juice from the frying pan, sprinkle with minced dill or parsley and serve at once.

Serve with mashed potatoes or new green peas as a side dish. Serves four to six.

MEAT BALLS IN TOMATO SAUCE (TEFTELI IN TOMATO SAUCE)

1 1/2 pounds ground chuck
1 bunch green onions
2/3 cup tomato purée
2-3 slices stale white bread
    without crust
2 tablespoons flour
2 tablespoons butter
1 cup meat stock or pre-
    pared consommé

1-2 bay leaves
5-6 peppercorns
2 tablespoons dill or parsley,
    minced very fine
Salt and pepper according to
    taste

Chop one bunch of green onions very fine and mix it thoroughly with the ground beef. Roll small meat balls on a board or a table top covered with flour, so that each meat ball is completely covered with flour. Fry them quickly in butter on a pre-heated frying pan. Put the meat balls in a pan, add meat stock or consommé, tomato purée, bay leaves, salt and pepper, cover with a lid and cook slowly for 15-20 minutes. Just before it is ready, you may add a teaspoon of any sharp steak sauce (this is optional). Sprinkle with minced dill or parsley and serve with rice or potatoes, boiled or mashed. Serves four to six people.

If you like the taste of garlic and if you are not afraid of its after effects, you may use 2-3 small cloves of garlic rubbed in salt and add them to your tefteli together with the rest of the ingredients.

MEAT ROLL WITH MACARONI (ROOLET WITH MACARONI)

1 1/2 pounds ground chuck
2/3 pound macaroni or spaghetti
2-3 slices of stale white bread without crust

1 1/2 cups red sauce
2 tablespoons butter
Bread crumbs
Salt and pepper according to taste

Cook macaroni or spaghetti, and cool. Prepare the following: soak the bread slices in a small amount of milk or water. Squeeze the liquid out. Mix the ground beef with the soaked bread, add salt and pepper and spread the mixture on a napkin, soaked in cold water and squeezed dry. Spread the ground beef very evenly with the help of a broad knife or spatula to the thickness of about 1/2 inch, and length of 12 inches or more. Right in the middle of the beef-spread put macaroni or spaghetti lengthwise. Sprinkle with melted butter and carefully bring the sides of the beef mixture together, folding the napkin over it. Seal the top and brush thoroughly with the beaten egg.

Put in a long baking dish, the sealed side down, brush with the egg and sprinkle with the bread crumbs. Make several pricks with a fork and bake in a moderate oven (350°) for

30-40 minutes. After about fifteen minutes of baking, sprinkle the top with a little more melted butter.

When roolet is ready, put it on a platter and cut into serving portions. Pour red sauce over the dish.

RED SAUCE

2 cups meat stock or pre-
    pared consommé
1/4 cup tomato purée
1 tablespoon flour
1 carrot, sliced
1 onion, sliced

1 sprig of celery
1 1/2 tablespoons butter
3-4 peppercorns
2 tablespoons dry Sherry or
    Madeira wine
Salt, according to taste

Sauté carrots, onions and celery in butter for a few minutes or until golden. In a separate pan, quickly fry flour in butter until dark brown. Add tomato purée and meat stock. Mix thoroughly. Combine with the vegetables and cook on a small fire for 20-30 minutes. Add salt and pepper and wine. Strain through a fine strainer and pour over the roolet.

ROOLET Stuffed with Rice and Egg

You may stuff your roolet with cooked rice mixed with hard-boiled eggs following the same directions and using the same RED SAUCE.

ROOLET Stuffed With Mushrooms

Follow the same recipe for roolet only stuff it with one pound sautéed mushrooms and onions. Serve with the same RED SAUCE.

FRIED CALF BRAINS I

2 pounds calf brains	6 peppercorns
Juice of 1 lemon	2 tablespoons dill or parsley,
4 tablespoons butter	minced
2 tablespoons vinegar	Salt and pepper, according
3 bay leaves	to taste

Place the calf brains in cold water for 30-40 minutes, then, take the brains out, remove the skin and possible blood clots. Put the brains into the pan with just enough water to have them covered. Add vinegar, bay leaves, peppercorns, bring to a quick boil. Then, reduce heat and continue to cook slowly for 25-30 minutes.

When the brains are ready, drain them, cut each section of the brains into two parts, sprinkle with salt and pepper, roll in flour on all sides and fry in butter on a pre-heated skillet.

When the brains are fried, put them on a pre-heated platter, sprinkle with melted butter and lemon juice and minced dill or parsley.

As a side dish serve mashed potatoes or green peas or french-cut beans. Serves four to six people.

BREADED CALF BRAINS II

Use the same ingredients and prepare the brains the same way as described in the preceding recipe.

The only difference is that after you roll the brains in flour, dip them into one slightly beaten egg and roll them in one cup of sifted bread crumbs.

Then, fry the brains in well-heated butter for 8-10 minutes until golden brown.

Put the brains on a pre-heated platter and sprinkle with minced dill or parsley, melted butter and lemon juice.

Serve at once with new green peas or french-cut beans.

VEAL ZRAZY

1 1/4 pounds fillet of veal (or   2 tablespoons tomato purée
    chunk of veal roast,   2/3 cup milk
    without bone)   3 tablespoons butter
1 1/4 cups meat stock or   Salt and pepper, according
    canned consommé   to taste
1 large onion, chopped fine
2-3 slices of stale white
    bread, without crust

Slice fillet of veal or veal roast into several slices, the size of your palm. Pound them slightly with a meat mallet.

Prepare the following stuffing:

Sauté the onions in butter. Soak the slices of bread in milk and squeeze them dry. Mix with the sautéed onions, salt and pepper and fry over a small fire for 2-3 minutes.

Put 1 tablespoon of stuffing on each slice of veal, roll them into small tubes and tie each tube with a string.

Fry each tube quickly in butter over a hot fire until each side is browned. Turn down the fire, add the meat stock or consommé and tomato purée and cook slowly under lid for 40-50 minutes, or until tender.

When ready, cut off the strings and serve with sharp tomato sauce. If there is enough juice left after the simmering, pour it over the zrazy and serve the sharp tomato sauce separately, in a gravy bowl. As a side dish, serve boiled white rice or new green peas.

GEORGIAN SOLYANKA (GROOZINSKAYA SOLYANKA)

1 1/4 pounds round steak
1/3 cup dry Sherry wine
2 dill pickles, sliced
2 onions, chopped
2 tablespoons tomato purée
3 tablespoons butter

1 small clove garlic
3 tablespoons meat stock or canned consommé
Salt and pepper, according to taste

Cut meat into one-inch-thick cubes. Remove all gristle and fat. Fry quickly in butter together with chopped onions. Place in a pot, combine with tomato purée, sliced dill pickles, clove of garlic, salt and pepper, meat stock and wine.

Cover with a lid and simmer for 30-40 minutes.

Just before serving, sprinkle the top with one tablespoon of minced parsley or dill (optional).

Serve hot, with boiled new potatoes as a side dish.

Serves four to six people.

FRIED STEAK WITH EGG A LA HAMBURG

4-6 small fillets of beef
3-4 tablespoons butter
4-6 eggs

Dill or parsley, minced
Salt and pepper, according to taste

Slightly beat the fillets with a meat mallet. Sprinkle with salt and pepper on each side. Fry in butter on a pre-heated skillet until both sides are browned. In a separate skillet fry eggs, sunny-side up.

Put one egg on each fillet, pour juice from fried meat over, and sprinkle with dill or parsley.

As a side dish serve buttered potatoes and green peas.

Serves four to six people.

I remember that this Beef Steak à la Hamburg was always a most popular dish on Russian restaurant menus—and for one simple reason: you could never be sure whether the meat would be tough or tender. So we, the Russians, gambled that even if the meat might be tough, at least we would have a sunny-side up egg to help us swallow the disappointment (and the steak!).

VEAL OR PORK OR LAMB CHOPS WITH MUSHROOMS AND TOMATOES

8-12 kidney chops of veal or pork or lamb
16-24 mushroom caps
4-6 small, firm tomatoes
8 tablespoons butter

1 clove garlic, chopped very fine
Salt and pepper according to taste

Beat the chops slightly with a meat mallet and sprinkle with salt and pepper. Fry on both sides in four tablespoons of pre-heated butter until ready (about 8-10 minutes). Or, you may broil the chops under a hot flame for about 5 minutes for each side.

Fry the mushroom caps (or sliced mushrooms) in two tablespoons of butter. Remove the skin from the tomatoes and slice them into two parts each. Fry quickly in the remaining butter.

Put two mushroom caps on each chop (or an appropriate amount of sliced mushrooms), together with 1/2 tomato.

Pour over it hot tomato sauce, with a little chopped garlic added to it. Serve two chops for each portion and as a side dish, serve hot boiled potatoes.

Serves four to six people.

KOTLETY WITH MILK SAUCE

1 1/4 pounds ground chuck
4 slices stale white bread,
without crust
2/3 cup milk
3 tablespoons butter

2 tablespoons grated cheese
1 tablespoon flour
Salt and pepper, according
to taste

Soak bread slices in milk and squeeze dry. Save milk for making the sauce. Mix soaked bread with ground meat, add salt and pepper and make oval kotlety, about 3 1/2 inches long.

Prepare the following sauce:

Dissolve flour in the remaining milk, add one tablespoon butter and cook the mixture slowly until it thickens. Remove from the fire and cool slightly.

Put the kotlety into a baking dish, making sure that the sides of the kotlety do not touch one another.

With a teaspoon, make an indentation along the length of each kotlety and fill it with the milk sauce. Sprinkle grated cheese and melted butter generously over each kotlety and bake in a moderate to hot oven for 10-20 minutes or until ready.

Just before serving, pour over kotlety the juice from baking, or red sauce (see p. 88).

As a side dish serve string beans or green peas or asparagus in milk sauce (in such case, double the recipe for the sauce).

Serves four to six people.

BAKED GROUND BEEF AND POTATOES
(ZAPEKANKA WITH MEAT)

3/4 pound ground beef
1 1/2 pounds potatoes, sliced
3 eggs
2 onions
1 tablespoon tomato purée

1/3 cup milk
2 tablespoons butter
Salt and pepper, according to taste

Slightly brown meat in butter and, in a separate skillet, sauté onions. Mix meat with onions, add tomato purée, salt and pepper, and a little water or meat stock. Cook under lid on a slow fire for 15-20 minutes.

Meanwhile, slightly fry potatoes, sliced rather thinly. Sprinkle with salt. Grease a baking dish and line its bottom with fried potatoes. Put meat and onion mixture over the potatoes and smooth the surface. Beat eggs with milk and pour this over the meat and potatoes.

Bake in a moderate to hot oven for 5-10 minutes, or until ready and the top of zapekanka is golden brown.

Sprinkle the top with finely chopped dill or parsley (optional).

Serves four to six people.

POULTRY

We make many interesting dishes from poultry, which is one of the favorite main dishes of every Russian.

I am giving here only the most interesting, neglecting completely such recipes as fried chicken or whole broiled chicken or broiled turkey. We prepare these dishes just as they are prepared in America, so there is nothing Russian about them. They are international dishes.

However, here are a few "secrets" which might help you to prepare even the most popular poultry dishes:

1. If you have to singe the chicken or turkey, have the carcass drenched in flour *before* singeing. It saves the skin from tearing and also prevents the carcass from smudging with soot.

2. When broiling a whole chicken, if you want a crisp,

rosy crust, have it covered with a thin layer of sour cream and sprinkled with seasoning before placing it in the oven. After that, baste according to your usual practice.

3. Serving chicken in wine, or with wine sauce, use only light white wine, like Sherry. However, if you serve any kind of game in wine, or with wine sauce, use Madeira wine.

4. Some people don't like the smell of broiling turkey. Place a small piece of fresh ginger inside the breast cavity before stuffing the bird.

5. For those who hunt small wild game, the Russians have an easy way of broiling the "daily limit." Clean the birds without plucking. Cut off the heads. Place a small slice of butter inside each bird and season with salt and pepper. Tightly sew the openings and cover each carcass completely with a thick layer of clay. Place the carcasses in the hot coals of the campfire.

When the clay dries and cracks the game will be ready. Remove the clay (the feathers will be stuck to it) and enjoy the most delicious and juicy wild game you've ever tasted.

6. If you are making soup from the bones of wild game, don't use the backs, for they will give a bitter taste to the soup.

7. Serving kotlety à la Kiev, have toothpicks at each plate so that your guests may prick the kotlety before cutting into them and thus avoid being splattered with hot butter.

CHICKEN FRIED IN BREAD CRUMBS

1 stewing chicken
2/3 cup coarse bread crumbs
1 egg
2 tablespoons flour
4-5 tablespoons butter
Salt and pepper, according to taste

Boil chicken in four cups of water together with usual soup greens (whole onion, 1-2 whole carrots, sprig of celery, bay leaf, 4-6 peppercorns, and so forth). Save the stock for further use. It will keep in the refrigerator for days, and it can be frozen, too.

Cut chicken into serving pieces, sprinkle with salt and pepper and roll in flour. Beat egg with a little cold water and dip chicken pieces in it. Pre-heat butter and keep it hot but do not burn. Roll the chicken pieces in bread crumbs and fry in butter for 4-5 minutes on each side. When ready, place the chicken on a platter, pour over it the remaining butter and decorate with choice sprigs of parsley (optional). As a side dish serve green salad or fluffy white rice.

Serves four and if you s-t-r-e-t-c-h it, it might serve six people.

KOTLETY A LA KIEV

One of the most famous Russian chicken dishes. Beware of the juiciness of kotlety, for many a frock has been ruined by those who cut into their kotlety too vigorously and allowed the hot butter to splatter all over them!

Kotlety à la Kiev are very attractive to look at and are delicious in flavor. They make a marvelous dish for informal, sit-down dinners, for they have the appearance of a very fancy dish, while being in reality very easy to prepare.

6 breasts of young chicken or capon
1/2 pound sweet butter, thoroughly chilled
2 eggs, beaten with a little cold water

Flour
Bread crumbs
Salt and pepper, according to taste

Cut the chicken breasts lengthwise and dispose of all sinews and skin. Pound the breasts with a meat mallet into very thin cutlets. Sprinkle with salt and pepper.

Cut cold butter into six pieces, one for each breast of chicken, and roll the butter into little fat rolls. Make sure that the butter is thoroughly cold all the time. Place the butter rolls in the middle of each chicken breast and wrap the cutlet around the butter rolls completely. Skewer the cutlets around the butter, making sure that the melted butter won't leak through.

Roll kotlety in flour, dip into eggs beaten with water, and then roll them in bread crumbs. The kotlety should be shaped into attractive narrow ovals and this requires some practice, so don't be discouraged if your first kotlety doesn't look too perfect.

Pre-heat frying shortening for deep frying and fry kotlety in deep fat for 2-3 minutes, or until just golden brown.

Drain, and place kotlety in a hot oven for 5-10 minutes more. Serve immediately, with wedges of lemon and new green peas. To make the kotlety à la Kiev look really festive, serve the green peas in little pastries, made of short dough, which you can buy in any bakery shop ready made (or you might make them yourself). Shoe-string potatoes look (and taste) quite good too.

Serves six people.

SPICY CHICKEN CASSEROLE (TCHAKHOKHBILI)

Tchakhokhbili of chicken is another famous Russian dish. To be exact, tchakhokhbili is a Georgian dish, but since the

Russians are notorious for appropriating other people's good ideas and calling them their own and, in the process, sincerely believing that they originated them in the first place— let's call tchakhokhbili a Russian dish.

Tcha-khokh-bi-li (it is difficult to pronounce even for a Russian!) used to be a favorite dish of the late Josef Stalin, but don't let this fact prejudice you against trying this dish. In my autobiography, *Kyra,* published by Prentice-Hall in 1959, I describe a lavish dinner at the home of young Stalin, the son of the dictator, where the main dish was tchakhokhbili. For those who have read *Kyra* and learned all the spicy details about the young Stalin, but wondered about the recipe of tchakhokhbili I highly recommend this one, and for those of you who have the recipe of this spicy dish right here, but wonder about the spicy details, I sincerely recommend that you obtain a copy of *Kyra* and find out for yourselves what kind of a "dish" this young man was.

Breasts, thighs and drumsticks of 2 chickens	4 small, firm tomatoes, quartered
2 onions	1 lemon, sliced very thin
3 tablespoons wine (Madeira or Dry Port)	2 tablespoons minced dill or parsley
1 tablespoon vinegar	Salt and pepper, according to taste
2-3 tablespoons tomato purée	
3-4 tablespoons butter	
1/3 cup meat stock or canned consommé	

Wash and dry the pieces of chicken. Pre-heat butter and slightly brown the pieces of chicken in it. Place chicken in a pot and add chopped onions, vinegar, wine, tomato purée, meat stock, salt, and pepper. Cook over a slow fire, under a lid, for 1 1/2 hours. During the last 5-8 minutes of cooking, add fresh tomatoes, with their skins previously removed.

Place the pieces of tchakhokhbili on a pre-heated platter and put a round slice of lemon on each piece of chicken. Sprinkle generously with dill or parsley.

Serve fine, wild rice as a side dish (or a plain white rice).

Serves four to six people. (Tastes just as good next day, reheated!)

Variation on a theme:

For those, who like mushrooms, you may add a few sautéed mushrooms to the basic recipe above.

CHICKEN KOTLETY

1 large stewing chicken	Milk
2 eggs	Coarse bread crumbs
8 slices of stale white bread, without crust	Salt and pepper, according to taste
5 tablespoons butter	

Soak bread in milk. Squeeze dry. Cut all meat from the raw chicken, removing all sinews, bones and skin. Put the meat through a grinder. Mix with the bread and add one egg. Mix thoroughly and force through a sieve. Melt butter and add to the mixture together with salt and pepper. Knead with your hands like a dough and shape into small cutlets. Dip each cutlet into egg, beaten with a little water and roll in bread crumbs. Fry in pre-heated butter or other shortening, using generous amounts of it. Serve at once with any kind of side dish, which goes with the chicken.

Serves four to six people.

These chicken kotlety taste very good even cold, sliced lengthwise, in a sandwich.

RAGOUT WITH CHICKEN GIBLETS

1 1/4 pounds assorted
   chicken giblets
1 1/2 pounds potatoes
1 onion
2 carrots
2/3 cup tomato purée

2 tablespoons butter
1 tablespoon flour
2 cups chicken stock or water
Salt and pepper, according
   to taste

Wash the giblets well and cut off all sinews, fat and skin. Cut into medium-sized chunks and fry slightly in butter. Sprinkle the flour over the giblets, shake well, and fry a little bit more.

Place the giblets in a pot, add chicken stock or water, add tomato purée, cover with a lid and cook over a slow fire for 1/2 hour. Meanwhile, prepare the vegetables. Slice the vegetables into medium-sized slices, fry them slightly in butter and add to the chicken giblets. Mix very carefully, so as not to break the chicken livers, add bay leaf and continue to cook over a slow fire for another 1/2 hour.

Serves four to six people.

STEWED CHICKEN WITH RICE UNDER
WHITE SAUCE

1 large stewing chicken
4 cups water
3 cups cooked rice
3 onions
3 carrots
1 stalk celery
2 tablespoons flour

2-3 tablespoons butter
1 small bunch of parsley
1 cup sour cream
1 tablespoon lemon
Salt and pepper, according
   to taste

Combine all the vegetables and place them in a pot and add water. Bring to a quick boil and add whole chicken, which has been washed and singed. Cook over a hot flame for 10-15 minutes, then reduce heat, cover with a lid and cook over slow flame for one hour, or until tender. Remove the chicken from the stock and thoroughly strain the stock.

Prepare the following white sauce:

Measure 2 cups of hot chicken stock. Melt butter and add flour; stirring constantly, let the flour turn slightly golden. Do not allow flour to brown, for then you'll have a brown sauce instead of white (however, it won't affect the taste). Slowly add chicken stock, stirring all the time. Add salt and pepper, lemon juice and continue stirring, simmer for 10-15 minutes. Just before serving, add sour cream.

Place chicken on a pre-heated platter. You may cut the chicken into serving pieces or leave it whole. If you leave it whole, arrange rice all around it, so that when you cut the chicken at the table, the rice will absorb the juice. If you serve the chicken pre-cut, you may pile the rice at the opposite end of the platter.

Pour the hot white sauce over the whole dish and serve at once.

Serves four to six people and it can be re-heated the next day without losing its flavor.

DUCK WITH CABBAGE (OOTKA S KAPOOSTOI)

1 large fat duck
1 head of cabbage, medium-
   sized
1 large carrot
1 large onion
1 leek

2-3 sprigs parsley
2 bay leaves
5-6 peppercorns
Salt and pepper, according
   to taste
Cracker meal or corn meal

For the sauce:

1 cup sour cream	*1 tablespoon butter*
1 cup duck stock, strained twice	*Salt and pepper, according to taste*
2 tablespoons flour	

Boil whole cabbage in salted water for 15-20 minutes. Drain and cool. Combine all the vegetables with duck in a large pot. Cover with boiling water and simmer for 1 and 1/2 to 2 hours or until the duck is tender. Remove duck, drain and strain the duck stock twice. Cut all the meat from the carcass and slice it into uniform chunks. Cut the cooled cabbage into uniform sections. Grease a large baking casserole dish and place the duck chunks in a mound in the center of the baking dish. Arrange the cabbage sections around the duck and sprinkle over it the cracker or corn meal.

Prepare the following sauce:

Melt butter and add flour. Stir constantly until the flour begins to change its color. Slowly add duck stock, stirring well. When thoroughly combined, add sour cream and mix well. Do not allow to boil.

Pour the sauce over the duck and cabbage and place in a moderate oven (350°) and bake for 25-30 minutes.

As a side dish, serve green salad or spicy apples. Serves four to six people. This recipe can be used in preparing a goose, too. In such case, use a large head of cabbage, double the amount of vegetables and double the amounts of the ingredients of the sauce. You may need more baking time too, so keep a close watch over your goose and test it for readiness throughout the cooking and baking process.

Goose may serve six to eight people.

Both duck and goose taste very good even if re-heated next day.

RUSSIAN SQUAB IN SOUR CREAM

This recipe could be adopted for any wild or domestic fowl, like partridge, Cornish hens, pheasants, and so forth.

4-6 squabs
1 1/2 cups heavy sour cream
1/2 cup sweet butter
2 large firm tomatoes, peeled
1 tablespoon parsley,
  chopped fine
1 teaspoon chives, chopped
  fine

4-5 shallots, chopped fine
1/4 teaspoon dry thyme
Salt and coarsely ground
  fresh pepper, according to
  taste

Split the squab and flatten them by removing the breast bone. Wash the birds and dry them with a damp cloth. Melt butter in a large, heavy-bottomed skillet and place squab in it, breast side down. Sprinkle with salt and pepper. Sauté over a slow fire, turning often until tender and golden. Place on a pre-heated platter and keep warm either in a slow oven or a covered double boiler.

Meanwhile, in the same skillet, sauté the vegetables for 10 minutes, stirring constantly. Just before serving add sour cream and pour over the squab.

Serves four to six people and the recipe can be doubled or even tripled for serving at informal parties. The main thing is to have enough sour cream, for it adds its own particular taste to the game and makes this recipe typically Russian.

As a side dish serve boiled white rice or wild rice.

GOOSE STUFFED WITH RED CABBAGE

1 goose	*1 cup apple juice or apple*
1 head of red cabbage	*cider*
1/4 cup sweet unsalted but-	*Salt and pepper, according*
ter	*to taste*
1 tablespoon vinegar	

Singe and wash goose. Prepare the following stuffing: shred red cabbage and sprinkle with salt and pepper. Melt butter in a large pot and add shredded cabbage, vinegar and 2 tablespoons of apple juice or apple cider. Mix well and cook for 5-8 minutes.

Rub the goose inside and outside with pepper and caraway seeds (optional) and stuff with cabbage.

Roast in a moderate oven until tender, basting about every 15 minutes with the drippings from the pan and 1-2 tablespoons of apple juice or apple cider, each time adding fresh apple juice to what accumulates in the roasting pan.

Serve with baked potatoes and gravy made from the roast's own juice. Serves six to eight people.

CAUCASIAN PHEASANT (FAZAN PO KAVKAZKI)

Pheasant has always been considered a special delicacy by the people of Russia, be they Russians themselves, or the members of many minorities which populate Russia. The Georgians, who live in the mountains of Caucasus, are particularly known for being fond of pheasants and for having some wonderful ways of preparing them.

I don't know whether it is possible to get fresh, green, not dried nuts in the United States. It is very important that the nuts—almonds or walnuts or pecans—must not be dried, for the oils and juices of fresh nuts add their own peculiar taste to this exotic dish. However, if you can't get the green nuts unless you live on a farm, try ordinary, store-bought almonds or walnuts or pecans. The dish still will taste very good, except that it won't be "Caucasian"!

2 *young pheasants*	1 *lemon*
1 1/4 *cups green nuts—al-*	1 *teaspoon lemon rind*
monds or walnuts or	1/2 *cup Muscatel wine*
pecans, halved	1/2 *cup very dry Madeira*
1/2 *cup sweet, unsalted but-*	*wine or 1/2 cup very*
ter	*strong tea*
1 1/4 *pounds seedless white*	2/3 *cup chicken stock or*
grapes	*canned chicken con-*
1/2 *cup red or black grapes,*	*sommé*
seeded and halved	*Salt and freshly ground pep-*
3 *oranges*	*per, according to taste*

Prepare the birds as for roasting, and rub inside and outside with wedges of lemon. Grease a baking dish and place the birds in it, rubbing them generously with butter all over. Sprinkle with salt and pepper. Add the nuts, wine (and/or tea), grapes, lemon rind and bake in rather hot oven (450°) for 15-20 minutes. Reduce heat to 400° and continue to bake for another 15-20 minutes. Slice oranges very thin and place them on the top of the birds. Dot orange slices with butter. Reduce heat again and continue to bake for another 10-15 minutes in a moderate oven (350°-375°). Place the birds on a pre-heated platter and arrange the nuts and grapes around them. Strain the remaining juice and combine with chicken stock or chicken consommé. Bring sauce to a boil and continue to cook for 10 minutes. Keep the pheasants warm by placing them in the oven, with the heat turned off, while you prepare the sauce.

Pour the sauce over the birds and the nuts and as a side dish serve wild or fluffy white rice.

If the grapes are overripe or not too perfect, add them to the dish after you have reduced heat for the second time.

You may discard the orange slices if they failed to keep their shape, however, if they still look perfect, you may decorate the space around the birds with them, placing the most perfect grapes or nuts in the center of each slice of orange.

This dish is very unusual and is very appropriate for serving at small informal parties. The recipe can easily be doubled or tripled.

This one serves four to six people.

VEGETABLES

For centuries cabbage and potatoes have been the main items on Russian menus. Ingeniously the Russians invented many ways to serve these particular vegetables. Cabbage is served in soups, salads, main courses, as a stuffing for traditional pies; it is served boiled, fried, marinated and raw. It is beloved by all Russians.

The use of potatoes is more conventional. I don't think that the Russians have added anything new to the serving of potatoes.

1. When making a cabbage pie, always rinse a head of cabbage with boiling water before proceeding with the recipe. This prevents cabbage from tasting bitter.

2. For fresh cabbage salad, rinse the head of white or red

cabbage with salted boiling water and then proceed with the recipe.

3. Cook fresh green peas separately from other vegetables, if you are making soup. Add green peas to the soup only just before serving. Fresh peas have a very strong flavor of their own which will pervade if cooked together with the other vegetables.

CAULIFLOWER

Cauliflower is one of the favorite Russian vegetables. The Russians serve it in several ways—as an appetizer, as an additional vegetable dish or even as a main course in a vegetarian menu.

Try these two variations on the same theme:

1 large cauliflower
3-4 tablespoons mayonnaise
3-4 tablespoons grated
  cheese

Salt and pepper according to
  taste

Put cauliflower into salted iced water for a few minutes. Drain water and put cauliflower into rapidly boiling salted water. Boil for 5-7 minutes, or until ready. Drain the water, put cauliflower on a serving platter and spread mayonnaise over it together with grated cheese.

The second method involves exactly the same ingredients and procedures except for the cheese. Instead of cheese, grate one or two raw beets and mix them with mayonnaise. Cool cauliflower before spreading mayonnaise over it. The beets will give the dish a piquant reddish color.

Serves four if used as a main course or six if used as a second vegetable. Serves eight or ten if used as an appetizer.

Cauliflower Under Sauce

1 large cauliflower
2/3 cup milk
1 tablespoon flour
2 tablespoons grated cheese

2 tablespoons melted butter
Salt and pepper according to
taste

Cook cauliflower in rapidly boiling salted water until done. Drain the water and put cauliflower in a baking dish, stem down.

Prepare the following sauce:

Combine milk, flour, butter and one tablespoon grated cheese (save the other one for later on).

Pour the sauce over the cauliflower and put the dish in a hot oven (400°) for 10 minutes.

Sprinkle the top with the remaining one tablespoon of grated cheese and keep cauliflower in the oven for another 5 minutes. Serve hot. Serves four.

Cauliflower with Butter and Bread-Crumbs Sauce

1 large cauliflower
1/4 pound butter
1/2 cup bread crumbs

Salt and pepper according to
taste

Put cauliflower for a few minutes into salted iced water. Drain the water and cook cauliflower until ready in rapidly boiling salted water.

Melt butter and add bread crumbs to it. Allow the bread crumbs to turn golden. Add salt and pepper.

Pour the butter sauce over cooked and drained cauliflower and serve immediately. Serves four.

BAKED AND STUFFED YELLOW SQUASH
OR EGGPLANT (KABACHKY)

3 medium-sized yellow
*   squash or 2 eggplants*
3/4 pound ground beef
1/2 cup cooked rice
1 onion, chopped
2 tablespoons sour cream
2 tablespoons tomato purée

1/4 cup water
1 tablespoon flour
1 tablespoon butter
1 tablespoon minced dill or
*   parsley*
Salt and pepper, according
*   to taste*

Slightly brown ground beef in butter and mix with cooked rice. Sauté onions and add to meat and rice mixture. Add salt and pepper. Take skin off squash or eggplant and slice into 4-5 slices each. Take out the seeds.

Grease a baking dish and place slices of squash or eggplant in it. Fill the centers of each slice with prepared stuffing, piling the stuffing a little bit higher than the edges of the slices.

Prepare the following sauce:

Mix tomato purée, sour cream and butter. Dissolve flour in water and add to tomato purée mixture. Bring to a quick boil and pour over squash or eggplant slices. Sprinkle with salt and pepper and bake in moderate oven for 30-40 minutes.

Just before serving, sprinkle with minced dill or parsley. Serves four to six.

NEW POTATOES IN SOUR CREAM

2 1/2 pounds new potatoes
2/3 cup sour cream
1 tablespoon butter

1 teaspoon minced dill or
*   parsley*

Wash and peel new potatoes. Boil in salted water until ready. Drain, add sour cream and butter, cover with a lid and gently shake.

Place on a platter and sprinkle with dill or parsley. Serves four.

POTATOES IN WINE SAUCE

2 1/2 *pounds potatoes*
1 *cup white wine (dry)*
1/2 *cup meat stock or*
    canned consommé
1 *onion*

1/4 *cup chopped celery*
2 *tablespoons butter*
1 *tablespoon flour*
Salt and pepper, according
    to taste

Wash potatoes and boil them without peeling. Cool. Peel and cut into thick slices. Sauté onions and celery in butter. Add salt and pepper. Dissolve flour in lukewarm consommé or meat stock and combine with wine. Place over a slow fire and add potatoes and sautéed onions and celery. Cook until sauce thickens. If necessary, add more wine or consommé or meat stock. Serves four.

WHITE CABBAGE WITH CREAM

1 *head of perfect white cab-*
    bage
2 *tablespoons butter*
1 *tablespoon flour*

1 1/2 *cups sweet cream*
White pepper
Salt, according to taste

Cook the head of cabbage whole in salted water until almost ready. Drain. Cut into serving portions. Combine butter, white pepper and salt. Mix flour with cream and add to the butter. Add cabbage and cook slowly until the cabbage is completely done. Serves four.

VEGETABLES IN MILK SAUCE

The Russians like to mix several vegetables and serve them under all kinds of sauces. One of their favorite ways of preparing mixed vegetables is to serve them hot and under white milk sauce.

2 1/2 pounds mixed vege-
tables—carrots, pota-
toes, celery, turnips,
green peas, or any other
combination (what-
ever you happen to
have!)

2 tablespoons melted butter
1 1/2 cup hot milk
1 tablespoon flour
Salt and pepper, according
to taste

Wash and peel vegetables. Slice or cube them and cook in salted water until ready. Drain completely.

Prepare the following sauce:

Slightly brown flour in butter and carefully mix with hot milk. Add seasoning and cooked vegetables. Cook over slow fire for 10-15 minutes. Serves four.

GREEN PEAS WITH POACHED EGGS
AND CROUTONS

2 packs of frozen green peas
7 eggs
6 slices of white bread

1 teaspoon sugar
2 tablespoons butter
Salt, according to taste

Prepare the croutons by slicing bread into small cubes. Beat one egg with sugar and dip the bread cubes into it. Melt butter and quickly fry the croutons in it. Cook the frozen peas (or fresh ones) in salty water. At the same time poach the remaining six eggs. When the peas are ready, drain them thoroughly. Mix green peas very gently with the croutons. Put one poached egg over each serving of green peas and serve at once.

Serves six people.

PUMPKIN WITH RICE AND EGGS (BAKED)

2 1/2 pounds of cleaned
pumpkin (actual pump-
kin, without seeds or
skin)
4 eggs

4 1/4 cups milk
2/3 cup water
2/3 cup uncooked rice
2/3 cup sugar
Salt, according to taste

Cut pumpkin into very small pieces, combine with water and salt and cook until soft. Add milk and rice and cook for 25-30 minutes more. Cool. Beat eggs slightly with sugar and mix thoroughly with pumpkin and rice. Melt butter and add to the mixture, making sure that all the ingredients are thoroughly combined.

Grease the baking dish or form and place the mixture in it. Bake in moderate oven (350°) for 15 minutes or until the top of the dish develops a golden crust. Serves four.

CANNED CORN WITH BAKED APPLES
AND CROUTONS

1 large can of corn
1 onion
2 tart apples
2 tablespoons tomato purée

2 teaspoons sugar
4-5 slices of white bread
4-5 tablespoons butter
1 egg

Sauté onion in butter. Mix with tomato purée and salt. Add corn, thoroughly drained. Mix well and cook over medium fire for 5 minutes.

Meanwhile, slice apples into eight parts each, removing all seeds and cores. Bake apple slices in the oven until they are soft.

Slice bread into small cubes, dip them into egg, slightly beaten with sugar and quickly fry them in butter.

Mix baked apple slices with croutons and arrange them around the cooked corn, piled up in the middle of a serving platter. Decorate the top of the corn mound with a few sprigs of very fresh and green parsley, arranged as a "bouquet." Serves four.

SPINACH WITH CROUTONS AND POACHED EGGS

2 1/2 pounds fresh spinach
4-6 eggs
1 egg (for dipping the
   croutons)
1 1/2 cups milk
1 tablespoon flour } *for making MILK SAUCE*
1-2 tablespoons butter
Salt, according to taste

Sort and thoroughly clean and wash spinach, add just enough water to cover the tops of the spinach, cover with a lid and cook over hot fire until tender. Force cooked spinach through a sieve and mix with white milk sauce. (See p. 114.) Add salt, a little sugar and heat thoroughly, stirring constantly.

Prepare the croutons and poach the eggs. Place spinach on a large platter, arrange the croutons around it and put the poached eggs on top. Or place one poached egg over each individual portion of spinach.

Serves four to six people.

Many vegetarians among Russians have invented many tasty vegetarian dishes which even the dedicated meat-eaters have found worthy of consideration.

Here are several ways of preparing delicious kotlety, without a scrap of meat!

POTATO KOTLETY

2 1/2 pounds potatoes
2 egg yolks
2/3 cup flour

4-5 tablespoons butter
Salt and pepper, according to taste

Wash and peel potatoes and boil them until done. Drain and let them stand for 10-12 minutes to dry. Without letting potatoes get cold, mash them thoroughly. Add 2 tablespoons butter, egg yolks, salt and pepper, and mix thoroughly. Form into cutlets, roll in flour (or fine bread crumbs) and fry in butter on both sides. Serve with mushroom sauce. Serves four.

CABBAGE KOTLETY

2 1/2 pounds cabbage, without the center core
2/3 cup farina or semolina
2/3 cup hot milk
3 eggs

2/3 cup bread crumbs
3 tablespoons butter
1/2 teaspoon sugar
Salt and pepper, according to taste

Shred cabbage very fine and put into a deep pot. Add hot milk and cover with a lid. Cook very slowly for 30-40 minutes or until the cabbage is completely soft. Add to the cabbage farina or semolina, very slowly, constantly stirring, to avoid lumps.

Continue to stir and cook for some 5-10 minutes more.

Remove from the fire, add egg yolks, salt and pepper and sugar and thoroughly cool. When the mixture is cooled, form it into cutlets. Brush the cutlets on all sides with egg white and roll in bread crumbs. Fry in butter on both sides and serve with milk or sour cream sauce. Serves four.

CARROT KOTLETY

2 1/2 pounds carrots
2/3 cup Farina or Semolina
2/3 cup hot milk
3 eggs

2/3 cup bread crumbs
1 teaspoon sugar
3 tablespoons butter

Wash and shred carrots, place in a cooking pot and add hot milk, one tablespoon butter, sugar, dash of salt and cover with a lid. Stir often and watch that the carrots don't burn (cook over low fire).

When the carrots are tender, slowly add Farina or Semolina, stirring constantly, and cook over slow fire for another 8-10 minutes. Remove carrots from the fire, cool for 2-3 minutes and add the egg yolks. Mix thoroughly and cool. When the mixture is completely cool, form cutlets, brush with egg white, and roll in bread crumbs. Fry in butter on both sides until golden.

Serve with sour cream or milk sauce. Serves four.

TURNIP KOTLETY

2 1/2 pounds turnips
4 eggs
2 tablespoons butter, melted
1/2 pound white bread
    crumbs

1/2 teaspoon sugar
1/4 teaspoon Muscat nut,
    grated
Dash of salt
Water

Wash and peel turnips, cut into small chunks. Cover with hot water and let stand for 10-15 minutes. Drain the water, place turnips in a pot, cover with boiling water and cook until the turnips are soft. Drain and put turnips through a meat grinder. Add salt and sugar, melted butter, and beat in the eggs. Mix thoroughly and add bread crumbs and Muscat nut. Beat again until the mass is completely mixed. Form cutlets, roll them in (or sprinkle over them) bread crumbs and fry in butter on both sides. Serves four.

Serve with following sauce:

RAISIN AND SOUR CREAM SAUCE

1 1/4 cups raisins (seedless)	*2/3 cup sour cream*
2-3 cups hot water	*1 tablespoon flour*
2 tablespoons butter	*Dash of salt*
2/3 cup sugar	

Combine raisins, water, sugar and butter and bring to a boil. Reduce heat and cook slowly for 15 minutes. Add sour cream and carefully add flour, trying to avoid making lumps and stirring constantly. Bring to a quick boil and serve with the turnip kotlety.

CABBAGE SCHNITZEL

1 firm head of white cabbage	*3 tablespoons butter*
2 eggs, slightly beaten	*Salt and pepper according to*
2/3 cup flour	*taste*
2/3 cup bread crumbs	

Wash cabbage and remove the core. Cook in salted water until tender. Drain and let it dry a little. Very carefully take the head of cabbage apart, leaf by leaf, crushing gently some of the coarser veins of the leaves. Fold each leaf like an envelope, roll in flour, dip into beaten eggs, roll in bread crumbs on both sides and fry in butter.

Place the cabbage schnitzels on a pre-heated platter and serve with sour cream sauce or with plain sour cream, served separately. Serves four.

FRIED EGGPLANT WITH ONIONS

2 eggplants	*3 tablespoons flour*
2 onions	*1 tablespoon tomato purée*
3 tablespoons butter	*2/3 cup sour cream*

Cut off the ends, and scald the eggplants with boiling water. Slice into thin slices, season, and roll in flour. Fry in hot butter on both sides and, in a separate skillet, fry onions, sliced to make uniform rings. Place eggplant slices and onion rings alternately on a pre-heated platter and make the following sauce:

Mix tomato purée with sour cream, season, and put into the pan in which the eggplant was fried. Stirring constantly, bring to a boil and pour over the eggplant and onion slices. Serves four to six people and is excellent as a side dish for any main course or as the main course itself.

BRAISED POTATOES AND MUSHROOMS

2 pounds potatoes	*1 bay leaf*
1 1/4 pounds mushrooms	*2 sprigs celery*
2 onions	*Salt and pepper, according*
3 tablespoons butter	*to taste*
2/3 cup sour cream	

Wash and scald mushrooms with boiling water and slice them. Peel the potatoes, slice and slightly fry in butter. Slice onions and fry them in butter together with the mushrooms.

Place in a pot, fill with water to the top of the vegetables, so that they are just covered, add salt and pepper, bay leaf, and celery. Cover with a lid and cook slowly for 25-30 minutes. Just before serving, remove bay leaf and sprigs of celery and add sour cream. Sprinkle the top with minced dill or parsley (optional). Serves four.

BRAISED BEETS IN SOUR CREAM

1 1/2 pounds beets	*1 teaspoon sugar*
1 carrot	*1 tablespoon flour*
1 sprig of celery	*2 tablespoons butter*
1 1/4 cups sour cream	*Salt and pepper, according*
1 teaspoon vinegar	*to taste*

Wash and slice all the vegetables. Place in a pot, season, add vinegar, butter, and just enough water to keep the vegetables covered. Cook slowly for 45-60 minutes, watching that the vegetables don't burn. Meanwhile, mix flour with sour cream, add sugar, and combine with the vegetables. Mix thoroughly and cook for another 10 minutes.

Serve as a side dish to any main course. Serves four to six people.

VEGETABLE RAGOUT

This is a wonderful dish to prepare for a meatless day, or for those who like vegetarian menus. You may use any vegetables in preparing it and the more different vegetables you find, the more interesting will be the result.

1 1/4 pounds small potatoes
3 carrots
2 turnips
2 onions (or 3-5 small onions, whole)
1/2 head of medium-sized cabbage (or 1/2 head of medium-sized cauliflower)
1/3 cup string beans (if frozen—1/3 of a package)

2 tomatoes or 2 tablespoons tomato purée
3 tablespoons butter
1 tablespoon flour
2 1/2 cups meat stock or canned consommé
Salt and pepper, according to taste
3-4 whole cloves
1/2 teaspoon cinnamon
1 bay leaf

Wash and slice egetables. Slice cabbage or cauliflower into medium-sized chunks and cook separately until just about ready. Drain the water. Add carrots, turnips, beans, bay leaf, and salt and pepper. In a separate skillet, fry onions very lightly (if you use very small onions, keep them whole, but brown them in butter by rolling them from side to side of your skillet). Slice potatoes and brown them in butter. Combine with the rest of the vegetables. Add two cups meat stock or canned consommé. Cover with a lid and cook slowly for 15-20 minutes.

Fry flour in butter and add 1/2 cup of meat stock or canned consommé. Add sliced and skinned tomatoes or tomato purée and bring to a boil. Add cloves and cinnamon and mix thoroughly.

Combine with the rest of the vegetables and cook slowly for 5-8 more minutes.

Just before serving, sprinkle with minced dill or parsley (optional). Serves four to six people.

TOMATOES STUFFED WITH GROUND BEEF

8 firm medium-sized toma-
toes
1/2 pound ground beef
2/3 cup cooked rice

1 onion, chopped
2-3 tablespoons butter
Salt and pepper, according
to taste

Wash tomatoes in cold water, cut off the tops, saving them to cover the tomatoes later, as if with a lid; carefully remove the seeds and pulp of the tomatoes, without destroying their form.

Fry onions, ground beef and cooked rice in butter very slightly. Add salt and pepper and mix thoroughly. Fill tomatoes with stuffing, cover with tomato tops and place in a baking dish. Sprinkle generously with melted butter or with grated cheese (in such case, don't cover the tomatoes with their tops). Bake in a moderate oven (350°) for 15-20 minutes.

Serve with sour cream sauce and sprinkle over the stuffed tomatoes a little minced dill or parsley.

Serves four to eight people.

WHOLE HEAD OF CABBAGE STUFFED
WITH GROUND BEEF

1 head medium-sized, firm
white cabbage
1 1/4 pounds ground beef
3-4 slices of stale white
bread, without crust
1 cup milk

1 1/4 cups sour cream
3 tablespoons butter
1 cup meat stock or canned
consommé
Salt and pepper, according
to taste

Wash a head of cabbage, cut out the core (or stem) and the few outside leaves. Cook whole in salted water until almost ready. Drain and cool.

Meanwhile, prepare the following stuffing:

Soak bread in milk and squeeze almost dry. Mix with ground beef and put through a meat grinder. Add salt and pepper and melted butter. Mix thoroughly. When the cabbage is cool, carefully separate the leaves, putting stuffing in between them. When all the stuffing is used, fold the leaves back, to form a head of cabbage. Sprinkle with salt and melted butter and place in a moderate oven (350°). If the cabbage threatens to fall apart, tie a string around it for the duration of baking. Baste frequently by using a little meat stock or consommé.

Bake for 50-60 minutes. About 15-20 minutes before the end of baking, pour sour cream over the dish and reduce heat to 300°.

When the dish is ready, place on a pre-heated platter and pour over it the strained sauce from the baking dish.

Slice carefully into 4-6 parts, cutting vertically, like wedges. It is a very filling dish and it is usually served as a main course.

Serves four to six people.

POTATOES STUFFED WITH GROUND BEEF

2 1/2 pounds large potatoes (best of all, Idaho potatoes)
3/4 pound ground beef
1 egg
1 small onion, minced

1 tablespoon dill or parsley, minced very fine
2 tablespoons butter
Salt and pepper, according to taste

Wash and boil potatoes, without peeling, until half-ready. Drain and cool potatoes.

Prepare stuffing:

Mix ground beef and onion. Brown very quickly in butter. Add salt and pepper and dill or parsley.

Take the skin off potatoes, cut them lengthwise and carefully take out part of the potato, making a long indentation.

Mash the removed parts of potatoes (or put them through a meat grinder) and combine them with ground beef mixture. Add egg and mix thoroughly. Fill the indentations of the potatoes with stuffing and firmly press the potato halves together. Place them in a cooking utensil very tightly, and add a little water or meat stock or consommé. Cook until potatoes are completely soft over a very slow fire. Serve with sour cream or tomato sauce. Serves four to six people.

You may also try to use some other ingredients in stuffing the vegetables. For instance, you may try the following variations:

VEGETABLE STUFFING

5 carrots	*1 tablespoon minced parsley*
3 onions	*Salt and pepper, according*
2 tomatoes	*to taste*
1 sprig celery	

Wash and drain thoroughly all the ingredients. Chop them very fine and brown in butter, all except tomatoes.

Remove the skin from tomatoes and slice them. Mix with the browned vegetables and simmer for another 5-7 minutes.

Add salt and pepper and stuff whatever vegetables you were going to stuff.

MUSHROOM STUFFING

2 cups chopped mushrooms
1 large onion, chopped
2-3 tablespoons butter (or
    more)

Salt and pepper, according
    to taste

Sauté mushrooms and onion in butter (but in separate utensils). When soft, combine them and add salt and pepper. Stuff the vegetables with mushroom stuffing and follow the preceding recipes' directions as to the rest of the process.

RICE AND MUSHROOM STUFFING

2 cups pre-cooked rice
1/2 cup chopped mushrooms
2-4 tablespoons butter

1 onion, chopped
Salt and pepper, according
    to taste

Sauté mushrooms and onion separately, then, combine with the cooked rice. Add salt and pepper. Stuff the vegetables as mentioned above.

MUSHROOMS IN SOUR CREAM

1 1/2 pounds mushrooms
2 medium-sized onions,
    chopped fine
3 tablespoons butter

1/2 teaspoon salt
Pepper
1 tablespoon flour
1 1/2 cups sour cream

Wash, drain and slice mushrooms. Sauté in butter until tender. In a separate skillet, sauté onions until golden. Combine the two, season and sprinkle with flour. Mix thoroughly. Cover with a lid and cook over a low fire for 8-10 minutes. Add sour cream, stirring constantly. As soon as the sour cream is absorbed, remove from fire and serve.

Serves four to six people.

SAUCES

SAUCES FOR VEGETABLE DISHES

I. MILK SAUCE

2 cups milk
1 1/2 tablespoons flour
2 tablespoons butter

Salt and pepper according to
taste

Slightly brown 1 1/2 tablespoons flour in butter and gradually add hot milk. Cook the sauce on a slow fire for ten minutes. Add salt and pepper and serve with or over vegetable dishes.

II. SOUR CREAM SAUCE

1 1/2 cups sour cream
3/4 cup vegetable stock
    (save the stock from
    cooking vegetables)

1 1/2 tablespoons flour
1 1/2 tablespoons butter
Salt and pepper according to
taste

Slightly brown flour in butter. Slowly add hot vegetable stock, stirring constantly. Add sour cream and salt and pepper. Cook over a slow fire for five minutes, strain the sauce and serve.

III. Mushroom Sauce (Made with Dry Mushrooms)

1/8 pound dry mushrooms   *1 tablespoon flour*
2 cups mushroom stock   *Salt and pepper according to*
1 onion, chopped fine   *taste*
4 tablespoons butter

Wash and dry mushrooms and then put them to soak in three cups of cold water for 2-3 hours. Then, cook the mushrooms without salt in the same water.

Meanwhile, brown flour in butter and, in another pan, fry onion. Slowly add two cups of strained mushroom stock to the browned flour and mix thoroughly.

Slice the mushrooms very fine and combine with the fried onion. Mix and fry together once more very quickly. Add to the liquid and bring to a boil. Add salt and pepper and serve with any potato dishes or with meat loaves.

IV. Tomato Sauce

1 cup meat stock or water   *2/3 cup tomato purée*
1/3 cup carrots, chopped very   *2 tablespoons butter*
*   fine*   *1 teaspoon flour*
1/3 cup onions, chopped   *Salt and pepper according to*
*   very fine*   *taste*
1/3 cup celery, chopped
*   very fine*

Brown the chopped vegetables all together in one table-spoon of butter. At the end of the process, add flour and mix it well. Add meat stock or water and cook slowly for 5-10 minutes. Add salt and pepper according to taste and put the sauce through a sieve, forcing the cooked vegetables through. Add another tablespoon of butter and stir well. Serve over or with any vegetable dish.

V. Sauce with Eggs

1 cup meat stock or canned *1 tablespoon butter*
 consommé *1 tablespoon flour*
1/3 cup milk *Salt and pepper according to*
1 egg yolk *taste*

Brown flour in butter and add meat stock or consommé. Stir well and let it boil slowly for 10-15 minutes. Beat the egg yolk together with milk and add to the flour mixture. Add salt and pepper and serve with any vegetable dishes, or roolets.

You may substitute for egg yolk a whole hard-boiled egg, chopped very fine.

VI. Egg and Butter Sauce

2 egg yolks *Lemon juice*
2 tablespoons cold water *Salt according to taste*
1/3 pound unsalted butter

In a top part of a double boiler put water and egg yolks and salt. Beat with a wire-whisk and add butter, one little piece after another, without interrupting the beating process. Do not allow the mixture to become too hot at any time.

As soon as the sauce thickens, add lemon juice according to taste and serve with cooked cauliflower or asparagus or artichokes.

VII. Egg and Wine Sauce

3 egg yolks	Peel of 1/4 lemon
3 tablespoons powdered	Juice of 1/4 lemon
sugar	Dash of salt
1 cup dry white wine	

Cream the egg yolks with the powdered sugar, add lemon peel in one large piece and gradually add wine, stirring constantly.

Put the mixture in the top of a double boiler and cook slowly, stirring constantly until the mixture thickens. Take the lemon peel out and add lemon juice and a tiny dash of salt.

Serve with cooked cauliflower or asparagus or artichokes.

VIII. Bread Crumb Sauce

6 tablespoons butter	Dash of salt
3 tablespoons sifted bread	
crumbs	

Melt butter and add bread crumbs. Stirring constantly, let the bread crumbs turn golden. Add salt, stir again and serve over cooked cauliflower or asparagus.

SAUCES FOR MEAT DISHES

IX. Meat Juice Sauce

After roasting any large piece of meat, take off the fat from the remaining juice by throwing into a pan a few ice cubes. The fat will cover the ice cubes and you can dispose of them instantly.

Add to the remaining meat juice 1-2 cups of meat stock or canned consommé or even plain water. Bring to a quick boil and, reducing heat, continue to boil for two minutes. Strain the sauce through a fine sieve and serve with your roast.

If you like a thicker sauce, add 1-1 1/2 tablespoons of flour to the meat juice *before* you add meat stock and cook for three minutes, stirring constantly.

X. RED SAUCE

2 cups meat stock or canned
  consommé
1/4 cup tomato purée
1 tablespoon flour
1 carrot, sliced
1 onion, sliced

1 sprig of celery
1 1/2 tablespoons butter
3-4 peppercorns
2 tablespoons dry Sherry
  wine or Madeira wine
Salt according to taste

Sauté carrot, onion and celery in butter for a few minutes or until golden. In a separate pan quickly fry flour in butter until brown, add tomato purée and meat stock. Mix thoroughly. Combine with the vegetables and cook over a small fire for 20-30 minutes. Add salt and pepper and wine. Strain through a fine sieve or a strainer and serve with any meat dishes, or roolets.

XI. TOMATO SAUCE

1 1/4 cups meat stock or
  canned consommé
2/3 cup tomato purée
1 small carrot, sliced
1 small onion, sliced
1 small stalk of celery, sliced

1 tablespoon flour
2 tablespoons butter
1 tablespoon prepared sharp
  steak sauce
Salt and pepper according to
  taste

Brown vegetables in one tablespoon of butter together with flour. Add tomato purée and mix well. Add meat stock or consommé and cook for 8-10 minutes on a slow fire. Add salt and pepper according to taste, one tablespoon of butter and sharp steak sauce. Mix thoroughly. Strain through a fine sieve and serve with any kind of fried meat, or kotlety, or brains in bread crumbs.

XII. Sharp Onion Sauce

2 cups meat stock or canned
  consommé
2 onions, chopped very fine
2 tablespoons tomato purée
2-3 tablespoons table vinegar
1 tablespoon flour

2 tablespoons butter
1 tablespoon dill pickles,
  chopped very fine
Salt and pepper according to
  taste

Brown one tablespoon flour in one tablespoon butter. Add meat stock or consommé and mix well. Brown onions in butter, add tomato purée, salt and pepper and continue to cook for one minute. Add vinegar and chopped dill pickles and continue to cook slowly until the mixture reaches the consistency of sour cream. Add to the meat stock mixture and boil over a slow fire for five minutes.

Serve with any fried or boiled meats or with fried or broiled liver or kotlety, etc.

XIII. White Sauce

2 cups meat stock or canned
  consommé or chicken stock
1 egg yolk
1 tablespoon flour

2 tablespoons butter
Salt and pepper according to
  taste

Brown slightly one tablespoon flour in one tablespoon butter. Add 1 1/2 cups strained meat or chicken stock and cook for five minutes over a slow fire. Take the sauce off the fire. Combine egg yolk with 1/2 cup of cold meat or chicken stock, add salt and pepper according to taste and combine with the hot sauce mixture. Stir thoroughly and add one tablespoon of butter. Put back on a small fire and cook for just one minute, stirring constantly.

Serve over boiled chicken or veal or with boiled lamb or mutton or rabbit.

XIV. WHITE SAUCE WITH CAPERS

Prepare the white sauce as in the preceding recipe. When ready to serve, add 1 1/2 tablespoons of smallest capers.

Serve with any boiled meat or chicken dishes.

XV. HORSE-RADISH SAUCE

1 1/4 cups meat stock or canned consommé	*2 tablespoons vinegar*
	2 tablespoons water
3/4 cup sour cream	*1 bay leaf*
4 tablespoons butter	*5 peppercorns*
1 tablespoon flour	*Salt, according to taste*
2 tablespoons horse radish, grated fine	

Brown flour in one tablespoon of butter. Add hot meat stock or consommé, stir well and then add sour cream. Cook on a slow fire for 5-10 minutes.

Meanwhile, prepare horse radish by putting it in a small skillet together with 2 tablespoons of butter and simmering it for 2 minutes. Add vinegar and water, bay leaf and pep-

percorns. Put on a medium fire to let the extra liquid evaporate (for about 5 minutes), then, add to the flour mixture.
Bring to a boil, add salt and 1 tablespoon butter, stir, take
out the bay leaf and serve with any kind of boiled beef or
pork or lamb or tongue. This sauce also goes well with all
kinds of dishes made with ground meat, like kotlety, bitochki, zrazy, etc.

XVI. Sour Cream Sauce

*1 1/4 cups meat or vegetable
    stock
2/3 cup sour cream
1 tablespoon flour*

*2 tablespoons butter
Salt and pepper according to
    taste*

Brown flour in one tablespoon of butter. Add hot meat or
vegetable stock and mix well. Cook for 5-10 minutes over a
slow fire, stirring constantly. Add sour cream and continue
to cook for one minute. Add salt and pepper and one tablespoon butter.

Serve with any kind of kotlety, bitochki, zrazy or with
broiled or fried liver or roasted fowl.

XVII. Sour Cream and Onion Sauce

*1 1/4 cups meat or vegetable
    stock
2/3 cup sour cream
1 onion, chopped very fine
1 tablespoon flour*

*3 tablespoons butter
1 teaspoon Worcestershire
    sauce
Salt and pepper, according
    to taste*

Fry flour in one tablespoon of butter until golden-yellow.
Add hot meat or vegetable stock and sour cream and cook
slowly for 5-10 minutes.

Meanwhile, sauté chopped onion in two tablespoons of butter until golden. At the end of cooking the flour mixture, add sautéed onions and Worcestershire sauce. Mix well and add salt and pepper.

Serve with fried or broiled liver, all kinds of kotlety or bitochki or with zrazy or roolet.

XVIII. YELLOW TURNIP SAUCE

2/3 pound yellow turnips   1 teaspoon lemon juice
1 tablespoon sugar   1 teaspoon ground lemon
2 tablespoons butter   rind
1 egg white   Dash of salt

Cook the turnips until absolutely soft. Cut into small pieces, mash and put through a fine sieve. Add sugar and mix. Add butter and start to cook very slowly until the mixture is very thick. Take from the fire and cool. Add egg white and beat until the mixture is very light and fluffy. Add lemon juice and lemon rind and continue to cream until everything is completely mixed and creamy.

Serve with fried or roasted meat of any kind or with fried or roasted chicken or game.

XIX. DRIED PRUNE SAUCE (SAUCE TKEMALI)

1 pound dried prunes   1 tablespoon minced dill
3 cups water   Salt and freshly ground pep-
1 clove garlic, minced VERY   per, according to taste
    FINE

Cook prunes in water until tender. Cool. Take out the pits. Strain the stock in which the prunes were cooked. Force the prunes through a sieve. Add just enough prune stock to make the mixture look like a very thin sour cream. Add minced garlic, salt and pepper and dill. Bring to a boil, stirring constantly. Cool slightly and serve with chicken roasted on a spit or with shashlik or Karsky shashlik.

Save the prune stock (it will keep in the refrigerator for a long time) and use it as a stock for any fruit sauce.

SWEET SAUCES

XX. APRICOT SAUCE

1/2 pound apricots (dried)	*1/3 cup wine (Muscat or*
1/3 cup sugar	*Muscatel)*
1/3 cup hot water	*1 1/4 cups cold water*

Wash dried apricots, drain and place in a pot. Add cold water. Cook slowly, adding a little more water if necessary. When apricots are absolutely soft, force them through a fine sieve and put back in the pot. Add sugar and hot water, mix thoroughly and bring to a boil. Continue to cook for five more minutes. Remove from heat and add wine.

This sauce may be served either hot or cold.

XXI. FRESH BERRY SAUCE

1 1/4 cups fresh berries	*1 1/4 cups sugar*
(strawberry, raspberry,	*1/3 cup red or white wine*
red or black currants,	*1/3 cup cold water*
etc.)	

Wash berries and force them through a fine sieve. Place sugar and water in a pot. Bring to a boil. Take off the foam. Into this hot syrup add wine and smashed berries. Stirring constantly, bring to a boil. The sauce may be served either hot or cold.

XXII. Chocolate Sauce

1 2/3 cups milk (hot)	*1 tablespoon cocoa*
2 egg yolks	*1 teaspoon flour*
2/3 cup sugar	

Beat egg yolks slightly with sugar. Add cocoa and flour. Mix very well. Add hot milk, stirring constantly. Put over slow fire and continue to stir. As soon as the sauce thickens, remove from fire and strain.

XXIII. Red Wine Sauce

2/3 cup heavy red wine	*1/3 cup cold water*
1 cup sugar	*1 teaspoon lemon rind*
2/3 cup hot water	*1 teaspoon starch*

Combine wine, hot water and lemon rind. Bring to a boil. Dissolve starch in cold water and add slowly to the wine mixture, stirring constantly. Add sugar and, without removing from fire, continue to stir until the sugar is completely dissolved.

The sauce can be served either hot or cold.

XXIV. Vanilla Sauce

1 2/3 cups hot milk	*1 teaspoon flour*
2 egg yolks	*1 teaspoon vanilla*
2/3 cup sugar	

Beat egg yolks with sugar until light. Add flour and mix well. Slowly add hot milk, stirring constantly. Cook over low fire, constantly stirring. As soon as the sauce thickens, remove from fire and add vanilla. You may strain the sauce, but usually it doesn't need straining, for if you have kept stirring it during cooking, it won't be lumpy.

XXV. Raisin and Sour Cream Sauce

1 1/4 cups seedless raisins
2-3 cups hot water
2 tablespoons butter
2/3 cup sugar

2/3 cup sour cream
1 tablespoon flour
Dash of salt

Combine raisins, water, sugar and butter and bring to a boil. Reduce heat and cook slowly for fifteen minutes, then add sour cream and flour, stirring constantly to avoid lumps. Bring to a quick boil and serve. This sauce may also be served chilled.

THINGS MADE
OF DOUGH

It makes me shudder to read the directions in one of my old Russian cookbooks on how to prepare the oven for baking: "heat the stove for 3-4 hours" advises the cookbook. "Use only dry birch logs, cut into four chunks each." Imagine cooking on a wood-burning stove, pre-heating it for 3-4 hours for the right temperature for baking!

Nothing pleases me more than a good stove. I am very fortunate to have one of the latest models of O'Keefe and Merritt stoves, which makes baking or broiling, or any cooking, a cinch.

Many Russian baked goods are used as desserts. Koolichy,

the traditional Easter cakes, may be served as desserts, or as coffee cakes. Pirozhki or pirogi, if filled with fruits or preserves or with sweetened cottage-cheese mass, also may double as desserts or as tea or coffee cakes.

The same dough is also used for pirozhki or pirogi made with non-sweet filling. These may be served with soups or, sometimes, as zakoosky before dinner, or as a late snack, or, for a real Russian, any time of the day, in place of any meal!

The Russians are very fond of home-made baked goods. No holiday is a real holiday unless there is a pirog. No party is a real party unless there are dainty pirozhki. Try serving them at a cocktail party.

I have not included in this book any recipes for cakes per se. All cakes were adopted by Russians either from the French or the British or the Germans. The same applies to cookies. As I have mentioned before, I have tried to keep this book restricted as much as possible to purely Russian recipes.

Here are a few secrets which might help you to make better Russian baked goods:

1. When making yeast-rising dough, let it rise three times. First, when a small amount of flour is mixed with the dissolved yeast, second, when the rest of the flour is added, and the third time, when the dough is shaped into a desired form or placed in the baking molds or forms. I have given the exact procedure with each recipe.

2. Never let the dough rise in a hot place. The heat won't quicken the process of rising, it will only create a tough crust over the dough.

3. When the dough is placed in the oven for baking,

avoid unnecessary opening of the oven's door. If you don't have an oven with a glass in it through which to peek, don't peek at all for at least 10-15 minutes.

4. In order to have the baked product come out of the form without sticking to it, have the insides of the forms well greased and thoroughly sprinkled with flour (unless advised otherwise in the recipe).

5. To test the readiness of the baked bread or koolich or any other large-sized product, stick a toothpick into several places at the end of the baking process. If the toothpick comes out clean and dry, your baking is done.

6. When baking small pirozhki, the rule about not peeking doesn't apply: if you don't have an oven with a glass in it, you must open the oven or you might burn your pirozhki. Only make sure that you peek very carefully, without allowing too much cold air to reach your pirozhki.

PIROZHKI AND PIROGI

A true Russian (or anyone who's ever tasted real Russian pirozhki or pirogi) can grow rhapsodic just talking about them. There is nothing more mouth-watering than a platter of hot pirozhki or a large, oblong pirog, which are as traditional holiday dishes in Russia as turkey or baked ham are traditional holiday dishes in America.

Pirozhki are small pastries with all kinds of fillings. You can improvise to your heart's content with the fillings, but the most traditional ones are of ground meat, or rice and chopped eggs, or cabbage and eggs, or mushrooms, or fish. You may also make sweet pirozhki, stuffing them with all kinds of fruit, fresh or canned, with sweetened cottage cheese, with berries, with raisins and nuts, and so on.

Pirogi are large, oblong pastries, made of the same dough as pirozhki and with the same stuffings, only they are huge in size, about 12 by 18 inches. They are more difficult to make and they are more difficult to eat, particularly at a buffet-style party, when most people eat standing up. Besides, the dainty pirozhki are more attractive and I have found that they rarely remain on the platter for more than a few minutes. My guests, whatever their nationality, seem to agree that it is hard to beat the Russian pirozhki!

RAISED DOUGH

1 cake of yeast	*1/2 cup butter*
1 cup lukewarm milk	*2 teaspoons sugar*
5 cups sifted flour	*1 extra egg yolk*
3-4 eggs	*1 teaspoon salt*

Dissolve yeast in the lukewarm milk. Stir in one cup of flour and let it stand for one hour in a warm place. Beat the eggs slightly and add salt and sugar. Add melted but cool butter. Combine with the yeast mixture. Add the rest of the flour and knead thoroughly with your hands. Form the dough into a ball and put it in a large bowl, slightly greased. Cover with a clean towel and put in a warm place to rise for the second time. It will take from 3-4 hours to rise, so be patient.

If you are making small pirozhki instead of a huge pirog, pinch off a small amount of dough for each pirozhok (the singular of "pirozhki"). Roll into an oval or round shape,

1/4 inch thick. Put one tablespoon of filling in the center of the rolled dough and carefully seal the edges. Let pirozhki stand and rise some more for 12-15 minutes. Brush their tops with the egg yolk, diluted with a little water.

Slightly grease a heavy cookie sheet and sprinkle it with flour. Bake pirozhki in a hot oven (400°) for 12-15 minutes, then reduce heat and bake them for another 15 minutes, or until ready.

You may also fry these pirozhki in deep fat. Then watch them come up to the top of the pan, just like doughnuts.

FILLINGS
CABBAGE FILLING

5-6 cups cabbage, chopped fine	1 tablespoon dill or parsley, minced
2 large onions, chopped fine	1 tablespoon salt
2 hard-boiled eggs, chopped	Salt and pepper according to taste
4-5 tablespoons butter	

Chop very fine the inside leaves of a firm, white cabbage. Sprinkle with one tablespoon salt and let stand for 10-15 minutes. Squeeze the cabbage dry. Pour boiling water over it and let it drain.

Meanwhile, sauté the onions in butter. Add cabbage and some more butter and continue to sauté very slowly (without letting the cabbage get brown) for another 20-25 minutes.

Add chopped eggs and minced dill or parsley. Add salt and pepper.

Use 1 1/2 heaping tablespoons of cabbage filling for each pirozhok.

BEEF FILLING

1 pound ground beef
2 hard-boiled eggs, chopped
2 medium-sized onions,
   chopped
5 tablespoons butter

2 tablespoons minced dill or
   parsley
1 tablespoon flour
Salt and pepper according to
   taste

Sauté the onions until slightly brown in two tablespoons of butter. Add the remaining butter and meat and continue to sauté until the meat turns brown. Add salt and pepper.

Remove the meat from the pan and mix it with dill or parsley. Cool the meat. Sprinkle flour into the pan where the meat was sautéed and brown it slightly, stirring constantly with a fork. Add a little water and bring to a quick boil. Add to the meat and mix thoroughly. Add the chopped eggs and start filling your pirozhki.

MEAT AND RICE FILLING

2 1/2 cups cooked ground
   beef
1/2 cup cooked rice
2 hard-boiled eggs, chopped
5 tablespoons butter
2 onions, chopped

3 tablespoons sour cream
2 tablespoons minced dill or
   parsley
Salt and pepper according to
   taste

Sauté the chopped onions in butter. Add ground meat and continue to sauté for a few more minutes (8 or 10). Add rice, sour cream, minced dill or parsley and salt and pepper. Cool. Add chopped eggs.

Use one tablespoon of filling for each pirozhok.

GREEN ONION AND EGG FILLING

2 cups of green onions, chopped	4 tablespoons butter
4 hard-boiled eggs, chopped	Salt and pepper according to taste

Sauté the green onions in butter until done, but not brown. Add salt and pepper. Cool. Combine with hard-boiled eggs. Use 1 tablespoon of filling for each pirozhok.

MUSHROOM AND ONION FILLING

4 cups mushrooms, sliced very thin	3 heaping tablespoons sour cream
2 onions	Salt and pepper according to taste
4 tablespoons butter	

Sauté mushrooms in two tablespoons of butter, adding a little more butter if necessary. In a separate pan sauté the onions in another two tablespoons of butter. When both ingredients are tender, combine them, add salt and pepper and blend in the sour cream. Use 1 1/2 tablespoons of filling for each pirozhok.

SOUR CREAM DOUGH FOR PIROZHKI

3 1/2 cups flour	1 teaspoon baking powder
1 cup sour cream	1 teaspoon sugar
2 eggs	1 teaspoon salt
1/2 cup butter (or other shortening)	

Sift flour, baking powder, salt and sugar, several times. Cut butter (or shortening) into tiny pieces and work them into the flour mixture. Beat the eggs very slightly. Add sour cream and mix very well. When the mixture is smooth, add it to the flour and continue to mix. It is best to work the dough with your hands, however there are some excellent pastry blenders on the market and if you don't like the feeling of working with a sticky dough, the pastry blender will do the job for you. Roll the dough on a slightly floured board to a thickness of 1/4 inch. Use one tablespoon of your favorite filling for each pirozhok (if you use cabbage filling, put 1 1/2 tablespoons of it in each pirozhok). Brush the tops of your pirozhki with a mixture of slightly beaten egg and a little water. Bake on a greased and slightly floured heavy cookie sheet for 12-15 minutes.

PIROZHKI WITH SALMON AND RICE

Here is another way to prepare the dough for pirozhki:

2 cups of sifted flour *1/2 ounce yeast*
1 cup shortening *1/2 teaspoon salt*
4 eggs, slightly beaten *1 teaspoon sugar*
1/3 cup warm water

Dissolve yeast in warm water and combine with 1 cup of sifted flour, salt and sugar. Add 1-2 tablespoons of lukewarm water and cover the mixture with a towel. Let it stand in a warm (not hot) place until it doubles in size.

Beat the eggs slightly and combine them with 2 tablespoons of lukewarm water. Add the remaining flour and mix it with the eggs, beating the paste vigorously against a pastry board or a smooth table top. Pull the dough apart and knead it forcefully several times, until it becomes firm and quite smooth. Add melted (but not hot) shortening and the yeast mixture. Continue to knead until all the ingredients are well mixed. Put into a deep, large bowl, cover with a towel and let it stand in a warm place for at least 5 1/2 or 6 hours.

Pinch the egg-sized chunks of dough and roll them on a slightly floured board to 1/4 inch thickness. Use 1 tablespoon of filling for each pirozhok. Let the filled pirozhki stand for 1/2 hour before baking them at 350° for 20-25 minutes.

CHICKEN FILLING (KOORINY PIROZHKI)

Prepare your favorite dough recipe. Use the following filling:

1 large stewing chicken	*1 bay leaf*
4 cups of water	*1 onion, whole*
2 medium-sized onions,	*1 carrot, whole*
chopped	*5-6 peppercorns*
2 tablespoons butter	*Salt and pepper according to*
1 pint sour cream	*taste*
2 hard-boiled eggs	

Cook the chicken together with 1 whole onion, 1 whole carrot, peppercorns, bay leaf and salt and pepper. When the chicken is tender, remove it from the stock. Take out onion, carrot, bay leaf and peppercorns and strain the stock, saving it for later use as a chicken bouillon, to accompany your pirozhki, or as a stock for your favorite chicken-soup recipe.

Remove all the meat from the bones. Put the meat through a fine grinder. Sauté onions in butter until golden. Chop the hard-boiled eggs very fine and combine them with the ground chicken. Add onions, and salt and pepper (if necessary). Mix in sour cream.

Use 1 1/2 tablespoons of filling for each pirozhok. Brush the tops of your pirozhki with melted butter and bake in a moderate oven (350°-375°) for 20-25 minutes or until ready.

SALMON AND RICE FILLING

1/2 pound cooked salmon
2-3 hard-boiled eggs
1/2 cup mushrooms,
  chopped
1/2 cup cooked rice

1 small onion, chopped
2 tablespoons butter
Salt and pepper according to
  taste

Sauté onion in 1 tablespoon of butter. In another pan, sauté mushrooms in 1 tablespoon of butter. Chop salmon and hard-boiled eggs. Mix with mushrooms and onions. Add cooked rice, salt and pepper. Form pirozhki and brush their tops with melted butter or a mixture of one egg yolk slightly beaten with 1 tablespoon of water.

NAME-DAY PIROG (E-MYA-NI'-NNY PIROG)

Emyaninny, or name day, is a very special day in Russia. Actually, it is a religious day, celebrating the saint's day after whom one was named. Before the revolution the emyaninny was celebrated with more verve than a birthday, with all kinds of traditional foods, one of the most important of which was the following pirog.

Prepare your favorite raised-dough recipe.

Roll the dough on a slightly floured pastry board and form a large flat sheet of 1/4 inch thickness. Grease a square or oblong baking tin (about 1 1/2 inches deep). Sprinkle it slightly with flour.

Carefully line the bottom and the sides of the baking tin with the rolled crust, and fill with the following filling:

2 *cups cooked rice*	2 *cups cooked white fish*
1/2 *cup green onions,*	4 *tablespoons butter*
chopped	*Salt and pepper according to*
4 *hard-boiled eggs, chopped*	*taste*

Sauté onions in two tablespoons of butter. Cool them.

Spread a layer of cooked rice on the bottom of your pirog. Dot it with small chunks of butter. Spread over it a thin layer of sautéed onions, then a layer of hard-boiled eggs. Dot this layer again with small chunks of butter. Make the next layer of small chunks of fish, sprinkling over it a little fish stock if the fish appears to look dry, or dot with extra chunks of butter. Repeat the whole process until all the ingredients are used.

Make sure that each layer is properly seasoned.

Cover the filling with the top crust, rolled to 1/4 inch thickness and seal the edges, pinching them firmly together.

Brush the top of your pirog with melted butter or egg yolk, diluted with a little water, prick the top crust with a fork and bake in a hot oven (425°-450°) until the crust is golden brown.

MEAT PIROG

Prepare your favorite raised-dough recipe. Follow the steps describing preparation of the emyaninny pirog, but fill the crust with the following filling:

2 1/2 pounds ground beef	*6 tablespoons butter (or*
5 hard-boiled eggs, chopped	*more, for you don't want*
2 large onions, chopped	*your PIROG to be too dry)*
	Salt and pepper according to
	taste

Sauté onions and, in a separate pan, fry very slightly the ground beef. Combine the two, add salt and pepper. Cool.

Add chopped eggs and mix thoroughly. Fill pirog with the mixture and cover with a top crust. Prick the top with a fork, brush with melted butter and bake at 425° until golden brown.

Serve with clear soup or with borsch or by itself, as a main dish.

Russians like to have a few dots of fresh, unsalted butter, which they put inside their slices of pirog. But whichever way you're going to serve your pirog it will taste delicious!

The above-mentioned amount of filling is intended for a tin 12 by 18 inches wide and 1 1/2 inches deep. Cut the recipe in half if you use a standard square tin of 9 by 9.

PAPER-THIN PANCAKES (BLINI)

Blini is another traditional Russian national dish. Although blini is an inexpensive dish which could be made and eaten any time, Russians usually gorged themselves on blini during Maslyannitza, a week-long carnival-type holiday preceding the Lent.

Nowadays, when there are no religious holidays in Russia, the people still prefer to overindulge in blini during the week of traditional, if abolished, Maslyannitza—or "butter week."

The best blini are made of buckwheat flour, or a combination of buckwheat and white flour. However, whole-wheat flour also makes very good blini. The main requirement in making the best blini is having plenty of time and not hurrying the process of preparing the ingredients.

1 1/4 cups buckwheat flour	2-3 tablespoons butter,
3/4 cup white flour	melted
1 cake of yeast	1 teaspoon sugar
1 1/4 cups lukewarm water	1/4 cup of heavy sour cream
1 cup hot milk	or heavy sweet cream
2 eggs	Dash of salt

In a large bowl dissolve yeast in lukewarm water. Add 3/4 cup of white flour and 1/4 cup of buckwheat flour. Mix thoroughly and cover with a towel. Put in a warm (not hot) place to rise and let it stand for about 2 1/2-3 hours.

Add remaining flour and mix thoroughly. Let rise again for another 1 1/2 hours.

Add to the raised batter 1 cup hot milk and mix well. Watch out for the milk skin. If there is one, discard it immediately. Cool.

Meanwhile, beat slightly egg yolks, salt and sugar. Slowly add melted butter. Whip sour cream (or sweet cream) until very fluffy, but not stiff.

Beat egg whites until stiff and fold the egg whites into cream.

Combine all the ingredients with batter and let it stand for another 1 1/2 hours.

Without stirring or disturbing the batter in any way, carefully spoon out one tablespoon of batter for each pancake and fry little round pancakes on a hot and, preferably, cast-iron griddle, slightly brushed with melted butter.

Make sure that blini don't run together, for the batter is rather thin.

In Russia we use several small individual cast-iron pans at the same time and thus have our blini perfect and universal in size and form.

When blini are done on one side, brush or sprinkle them with hot melted butter and turn them over. As soon as the first batch is ready, stack them up on a hot platter and continue the process. It takes about 2-3 minutes to brown each side of the blini and they taste best when they are sizzling hot.

Serve with hot melted butter (a must!), sour cream, black or pressed or red caviar, or with thin slices of smoked salmon or sturgeon (but *always* with melted butter).

You may also serve blini with preserves or syrups.

If you have any leftover blini, stuff them with cooked ground meat and sautéed onions, roll into little tubes and fry in butter on both sides.

Or fill them with canned fruits or preserves, roll into tubes, fry in butter and sprinkle with powdered sugar.

Or use your imagination and stuff them with whatever's handy, fry in butter and enjoy 'm!

More likely, though, you won't have any leftovers!

The recipe above should make about 20-25 blini, serving three Russians but four to six Americans.

BLINI—NOT SO RICH

2 cups buckwheat flour
3 cups warm milk
1 cake of yeast
4 eggs

2 teaspoons butter, melted
1 teaspoon sugar
1/8 teaspoon salt

In a large bowl dissolve yeast in 1 1/2 cups of warm milk. Add 3/4 cup flour, cover with a towel and let it stand in a warm place for 2 1/2 to 3 hours.

Beat egg yolks together with sugar and salt. Add the rest of the warm milk and melted butter. Mix with the yeast mixture. Beat egg whites and add to the yeast mixture. Carefully fold in the remaining flour. Cover with a towel and put into a warm place for another 20-30 minutes. Pre-heat the griddle and brush it very lightly with melted butter (using a pastry brush or, as we do it in Russia, a feather).

Ladle 1 tablespoon of batter for each pancake (or, if you like them bigger—1/4 cup), brown them lightly on each side.

Serve with hot melted butter, caviar or smoked fish or with heavy sour cream.

Makes 25-30 blini.

VERY QUICK BLINI

These tiny blini make a perfect base for all kinds of cocktail spreads. As their name suggests, they are very easy to prepare and they can be offered to the guests as long as there is a demand for them, which, I dare to predict, will hardly ever end.

1 cup buckwheat flour	*1 tablespoon melted butter*
1 teaspoon baking powder	*1 teaspoon sugar*
1 egg, slightly beaten	*2 tablespoons sour cream*
3/4 cup lukewarm milk	*Dash of salt*

Sift together three times flour, baking powder, sugar and salt. Beat egg very slightly, add sour cream and melted butter. Blend well. Add lukewarm milk. Add sifted ingredients and mix thoroughly.

Fry in butter on a pre-heated griddle, making each cake no bigger than two inches in diameter.

Put the blini on the platter, top with one tablespoon of heavy sour cream for each pancake. Put 1 teaspoon of black or red caviar on the top of sour cream and serve at once. Serves 4-6 people.

Double or triple the recipe for larger amount of people. If caviar is not available, top your little blini with any kind of smoked fish or small chunks of baked ham, or with sardines.

Children love the little blini when they are topped with apricot or strawberry jam. I love them just with plain sour cream.

I. STUFFED PAPER-THIN PANCAKES (BLINCHIKI)

Blinchiki may be stuffed with all kinds of things and are very easy to prepare. They can be served with soup if stuffed with meat, or they can be served as an entrée or, if stuffed with preserves, they can be served as a dessert.

2 cups flour	1 teaspoon sugar
2 cups milk	Butter
2 eggs	Dash of salt

Beat eggs very slightly, add sugar and salt. Slowly add milk, stirring constantly. Very slowly add flour (1/4 cup at a time). Mix very thoroughly for the batter must be very smooth and thin. If it looks thick, add 1 or 2 tablespoons of milk.

Heat a heavy frying pan and grease it very lightly with butter. Fry, on one side only, thin pancakes 4-5 inches in diameter. Stack them on a platter and, when all the pancakes are fried, stuff them with ground fried meat, putting two tablespoons of it on the fried side of the blinchiki, rolling them into little tubes and frying them again in small amounts of butter. You may stuff blinchiki with slightly sweetened cottage cheese, or with canned and drained fruits or preserves.

In such case, after blinchiki are fried, dust them with powdered sugar and serve with heavy sour cream while they are still warm.

Blinchiki taste very good also when served cold. Besides, they can always be re-heated. Serves four to six people.

II. BLINCHIKI WITH APPLESAUCE

1 cup flour	*2 tablespoons applesauce*
1 cup milk	*1 tablespoon sugar*
2 eggs	*Dash of salt*
2 tablespoons butter, melted	

Beat together eggs, sugar and salt. Add milk slowly and flour. Blend in applesauce. Add melted butter. The batter should be very thin, so add more milk if necessary. Fry on a hot, heavy griddle or frying pan which has been greased lightly with butter.

Fry blinchiki on both sides, stuff them with preserves or more applesauce, and roll into little tubes. Fry them again in a little butter, or put them in a baking dish, close to one another, sprinkle with powdered sugar and melted butter and put in a moderate oven (350°) for 10-15 minutes.

You may also stuff blinchiki with cottage cheese mixed with 2-3 tablespoons of sour cream, or stuff them with ground fried meat and onions.

Always serve blinchiki with a generous amount of heavy sour cream. Serves four to six people.

STACKED-UP STUFFED BLINCHIKI (BLINCHATY PIROG)

Prepare the batter as for blinchiki #1. Fry them only on one side. Make the following stuffing:

MUSHROOM STUFFING

2 cups mushrooms, sliced
1 large onion, sliced
1 egg, hard-boiled
1 egg, raw and slightly
　beaten
Butter

2 tablespoons parsley,
　chopped very fine
2-3 tablespoons sour cream
Salt and pepper, according
　to taste
Bread crumbs

Sauté in two separate pans sliced mushrooms and sliced onion in small amounts of butter. Cool slightly and then combine. Add salt and pepper and fine-chopped hard-boiled egg. Add chopped parsley and blend in sour cream.

Spread a little butter on each pancake (on the unfried side) and put 2-3 tablespoons of stuffing on each of them, piling them up on top of one another, spreading the stuffing very evenly. Beat one egg very slightly and brush the sides and the top of your blinchaty pirog. Be generous and make sure that all the surfaces are thoroughly covered with beaten egg. Sprinkle with bread crumbs and bake in a hot oven (450°) for 10-15 minutes or until the pirog is golden brown. Serve with sour cream or just plain.

MEAT STUFFING FOR BLINCHATY PIROG

Use the recipe for blinchiki #1 in preparing the batter for this pirog.

MEAT STUFFING

3 *cups fried ground beef*
1 *large onion, chopped*
1 *egg hard-boiled*
1 *egg raw and slightly*
beaten
2 *tablespoons parsley,*
minced

Butter
Salt and pepper, according
to taste
Bread crumbs

Prepare the batter as for blinchiki #I. Fry them only onion in a small amount of butter. Cool them both and then combine.

Add chopped hard-boiled egg, parsley, salt and pepper, and mix it all thoroughly.

Butter slightly (on the unfried side) each little pancake. Spread the stuffing evenly on the unfried side of the first pancake, cover it with another pancake, so that the fried side faces the stuffing, and continue the procedure, stacking the pancakes on top of one another.

Brush the top and the sides of your stack of pancakes with slightly beaten egg and sprinkle generously with bread crumbs.

Bake in a hot oven (450°) for 10-15 minutes, or until the pirog is golden brown.

LIVER STUFFING FOR BLINCHATY PIROG

Prepare the batter for your pirog as in the recipe for blinchiki #I and follow the same procedure in frying.

Prepare the following stuffing:

2 1/2 pounds liver (baby beef is the best)

1 large onion

3 eggs, hard-boiled

2-3 tablespoons butter

2-3 tablespoons dill or parsley, chopped

Salt and pepper, according to taste

Bread crumbs

Cook the liver in a small amount of water, 1 bay leaf and a dash of salt. Drain the liver, cut liver into chunks, remove all the gristle and put the liver through a fine meat grinder. Chop onion very fine and fry it slightly in a small amount of butter. Combine the liver with the onion, add chopped hard-boiled eggs, dill or parsley, and salt and pepper. Mix it thoroughly. Grease the sides and the bottom of a small cake pan with melted butter, and dust with bread crumbs.

Line the sides and the bottom of the pan with the pancakes, the unfried side against the pan, and sprinkle with more butter. Spread the liver stuffing and cover with a pancake. Sprinkle with butter. Repeat the process until all the stuffing and all the pancakes are gone. Brush the top pancake with slightly beaten egg, sprinkle with bread crumbs and bake in a hot oven for 15-20 minutes.

VARENNIKI I

Delicious tidbits which can be a whole meal!

2 cups flour

1 egg yolk

2-3 tablespoons water

Sift flour three times. Beat egg yolk very slightly. Add water. Add flour and knead the dough very well. Roll the dough very thinly on a floured towel and cut into squares 3 inches in diameter.

Stuff with the following mixture:

1 cup creamed cottage	*Dash of sugar*
cheese	*Salt according to taste*
1 egg	

Beat the egg very slightly. Add salt and sugar. Add cottage cheese and mix thoroughly. Place one tablespoon of cottage cheese mixture on each square. Seal the edges securely, making neat little envelopes.

Drop varenniki into rapidly boiling salted water. Varenniki are done when they come up to the top of the water. Take them out of the water, drain, and put them on a platter. Serve hot together with melted butter and sour cream.

II. VARENNIKI (WITH FRESH FRUITS OR BERRIES)

This was always a favorite Russian dish during the summer, when fruits and berries were plentiful. It is a very inexpensive dish, and may well become the children's favorite.

2 pounds cherries or blue-	*1 cup sugar*
berries or strawberries or	*1 cup water*
plums or apricots, etc.	*4 egg yolks*
3 cups flour	*Salt according to taste*

Wash and pit berries or fruits. Cover them with sugar and let stand for one hour. Drain the juice and bring to a quick boil, after which continue to boil slowly for 10-15 minutes. If you are using cherries, crush and boil a few pits with your syrup. It will make it more aromatic. Strain the syrup and let it cool.

Meanwhile, prepare the following dough:

Beat slightly the egg yolks and salt. Add water very slowly. Add flour 1/4 cup at a time. Mix very thoroughly.

Roll the dough very thinly on a slightly floured towel and cut into 3-inch circles.

Place one tablespoon of fruit or berries on each circle. Moisten the edges with slightly beaten egg white. Fold the circles over and firmly press the edges together with a fork. Put varenniki into rapidly boiling salted water. When they surface, drain them, put on a platter, and serve hot with previously prepared syrup or with powdered sugar and sour cream. Or, you may serve them with melted butter and powdered sugar. Serves four to six people.

PELMENY SIBERIAN

Long before frozen foods were invented, Russians living in Siberia discovered their advantages. I don't know whether my compatriots have ever claimed being the first to invent frozen foods, but if they have, it must be one of those instances when they might have been right. For hundreds of years Siberians are known to have frozen their pelmeny for later use. The distances between one village and another being so great in Siberia, people often traveled for days without ever coming to a place of habitation. Thus they always carried enough food with them to last for several days. Frozen pelmeny, which they carried by sackfuls, was their favorite fare since it required practically nothing but a fire, a pot and snow, of which there was always plenty, to use instead of water.

Melting the snow, the Siberians would bring it to a boil and, throwing the frozen pelmeny into it, they would have a delicious and very nourishing meal ready in no time.

Pelmeny are delicious little meat pastries, sort of like tiny pirozhki which might be served with meat bouillon, or fried, or boiled in plain salty water and served with sour cream or vinegar or butter.

The best, real way of preparing Siberian pelmeny is to use two kinds of meat for stuffing—beef and pork or veal and pork—and plenty of seasoning.

1/2 pound ground beef	*2 cups of flour, sifted twice*
1/2 pound ground pork	*1/3 cup water*
2 medium-sized onions	*Salt and pepper, according*
1 egg	*to taste*

Combine ground beef and ground pork and put it twice through a meat grinder, together with onions. Add salt and pepper and one teaspoon water.

Prepare the following dough:

Beat egg slightly and combine with water. Add flour, dash of salt, and knead a rather dry dough. Roll the dough very thinly and cut out two-inch circles. Put a small ball of stuffing (about 1/2 teaspoon) into each circle and pinch the edges, making little half-moons. Pinch the corners of each half-moon together.

Have a meat bouillon boiling (or prepared consommé, using one can of consommé, prepared according to directions printed on the label, for each two people).

In order to keep the bouillon with pelmeny clear and transparent, have another pot with boiling water ready.

Dip pelmeny into plain boiling water for a few seconds, scoop them up and place in boiling bouillon or consommé.

When pelmeny are ready, they will surface like doughnuts.

Serve in deep soup plates, together with bouillon or con-sommé.

You may also boil pelmeny in plain salted water. In such case, when pelmeny are ready, drain them and serve with heavy sour cream or with vinegar and melted butter.

Or you may fry pelmeny in butter. In such case, don't boil pelmeny for more than two minutes.

You may also make a quick sharp sauce for your pelmeny, which the Siberians especially like: mix sharp mustard with fruit vinegar and pour over the plain pelmeny, boiled in salty water.

Serves four to six people. However, if you have Russians for dinner, you'd better double or triple the recipe. The minimum that a good, red-blooded Russian would require is one dozen of pelmeny and I have known Russians who could eat two or three dozen pelmeny at one sitting. I, myself, have eaten two dozen (regretfully, I must confess, I wasn't feeling too well afterwards!).

POPPY SEED ROLL

Prepare the dough, following the previous recipe. While the dough is rising for the second time, prepare the following filling:

3/4 pound poppy seed	*1 teaspoon grated lemon rind*
1/2 pound honey	*or 1 teaspoon vanilla*
1/2 cup sugar	*Powdered sugar*
1/2 teaspoon salt	

Place poppy seeds in a container and cover with boiling water. Cover with a lid and let stand for 30-40 minutes. Drain the water and slightly squeeze the poppy seeds. Crush them in a mortar or force through a very fine sieve. Gradually add honey and sugar until the mixture becomes thick but smooth. Add lemon rind or vanilla. Mix thoroughly.

Roll the dough on a slightly floured pastry board or a table top to the thickness of approximately 1/2 inch. Spread the poppy-seed mixture over the dough very evenly and roll the dough into a tube. Place the poppy seed roll on a slightly greased baking sheet, and place in a warm spot to rise. When it has risen, brush the top with an egg, slightly beaten with a little water, and bake in a pre-heated oven (425°-450°) for 20-30 minutes. Cool and, just before serving, sprinkle with powdered sugar.

WHITE BREAD (BOOLOCHKY)

Boolochky are little dinner rolls, of which the Russians can eat enormous quantities. You may use this recipe to make 2-3 dozen of boolochky or 2-3 loaves of wonderful bread.

2 1/2 pounds sifted flour	1/2 pound butter or margarine
2 2/3 cups warm milk	
2 eggs	1 ounce fresh yeast
1 egg for brushing the tops of boolochky	3/4 teaspoon salt
	1 teaspoon vanilla
1 cup sugar	

Dissolve yeast in warm milk and add one cup of flour. Mix until absolutely smooth. Cover with a towel and put in a warm place to rise. Do not put it in a hot place; it won't speed up the process and only will dry the top of the dough.

When the batter doubles in bulk (in about 2-3 hours), add salt, melted butter and vanilla. Beat 2 eggs with sugar until very light in color and add to the flour mixture. Knead the dough until very pliable. Cover with a towel and let it rise again. As soon as the dough doubles in size, put on a board slightly sprinkled with flour and make little rolls (or, if you are making bread, form oblong shapes and place them in bread-loaf forms. Be sure to have enough space at the tops of your forms to let the dough rise; in other words, fill the forms only half full).

Slightly grease the baking sheet and let boolochky rise again (or the bread in their forms). Brush the tops of boolochky or bread with slightly beaten egg and bake in a hot oven for 12-15 minutes (more for bread). The bread is ready when a toothpick stuck into it comes out absolutely dry.

If you like less-rich dough, cut the amount of sugar and butter in half. You can use this recipe in preparing any stuffed boolochky.

In such case, after you have shaped your boolochky, make small holes in the middle of each and fill the holes with apricot preserves or with strawberry jam.

You may also mix one quart of cottage cheese with six tablespoons of sour cream and sugar, according to taste, and use the mass for filling. Or you may use any meat fillings.

RAISED-DOUGH SWEET ROLLS (BOOLOCHKY-CHANEZHKY)

2 1/2 pounds white flour,
    sifted twice
1 3/4 cups milk
1 2/3 cups sugar
3/4 pound butter or marga-
    rine

5 egg yolks
1 1/2 ounces yeast
1/2 teaspoon salt

For brushing the tops of chanezhky:

1 tablespoon sour cream	*1 tablespoon flour*
1 tablespoon butter	*1-1 1/2 tablespoon sugar*

Dissolve yeast in warm milk and mix with half of the sifted flour. Cover with a towel and place in a warm (not hot) place to rise.

Beat the egg yolks with sugar and melt butter or margarine, just before the dough is ready for the next step. When the dough has doubled in size—add egg yolks and sugar mixture and melted butter and mix thoroughly. Add the remaining flour and salt. Knead thoroughly, until the dough stops sticking to the sides of the bowl. Cover with a towel and place to rise once more.

When the dough has doubled in size for the second time, place it on a slightly floured board or table top and form in small rolls. Place the rolls on a slightly greased baking sheet and let them rise again. Meanwhile, combine the ingredients for brushing the tops of chanezhky and have them ready. As soon as the rolls have risen, brush the tops with the sour cream mixture and bake in a moderate to hot oven (350°-375°) for 12-15 minutes.

You may use the same recipe to make white bread. In such case, use only 3/4 cup of sugar.

You may also use the same basic recipe for preparing the dough for the poppy seed roll.

ALMOND KOOLICH

Follow the previous recipe only use 3/4 pound blanched and shredded almonds and no raisins or candied rind of lemon or orange.

Add almonds to the dough after the second rising of the dough. Save 3-4 tablespoons of almonds to decorate the tops of your koolichy. Watch that the almonds on the top don't burn during the baking process.

Always cool your koolichy completely before removing them from the forms. Of course, you may use any kind of cake form or bread loaf form with this recipe—you don't have to stick to the traditional Russian tall form.

RUSSIAN TRADITIONAL EASTER CAKE (KOOLICH)

Russian traditional Easter cake, koolich, is always made in a tall form. I found that it is almost impossible to find a tall form in the U.S.A., unless you know some old Russian artisan who knows exactly what kind of form it has to be, to be authentic, and makes one for you. Thus, I was forced to improvise.

I have found that a two-pound coffee can makes an almost perfect cake form and that a three-pound can from any shortening makes an even better one. Russians always make several koolichy (plural of koolich) and they slice them horizontally, keeping the top crust part as a lid to cover the remaining koolich. Consequently, the koolich appears to grow shorter with each slicing, yet, on the surface, it keeps its original form.

Koolich keeps fresh and tasty for days if kept wrapped in wax paper and in the refrigerator. Even if koolich becomes dry, you can still enjoy it, sliced very thin, and slightly browned in a moderate oven for 3-5 minutes. In such case, you may sprinkle each slice of koolich with a little sugar or brush each slice with a little of your favorite preserve.

8 cups sifted white flour
1 3/4 cups warm milk (or slightly more)
3/4 pound butter or margarine, melted
6 eggs
2 cups sugar
1 1/2 ounces yeast
3/4 teaspoon salt

1 1/4 cups raisins
1/2 cup blanched and shredded almonds
1/2 cup candied lemon or orange rind or mixture of both
1 teaspoon vanilla or a 1/2 teaspoon cardamon

Dissolve yeast in warm milk and mix thoroughly with 4 cups of sifted flour, adding flour gradually and mixing thoroughly, until the batter is absolutely smooth. Cover with a towel and place in a warm spot to rise.

When the dough doubles in size, beat the egg yolks with sugar very lightly, add vanilla, and combine with batter. Beat the egg whites until stiff and fold into the batter mixture. Add the remaining four cups of flour and melted butter. Continue to mix until the batter is completely mixed and is very smooth. Cover with a towel and put in a warm place to rise. When the dough doubles in size again, add raisins, almonds and candied lemon or orange rind. Mix thoroughly and fill the forms half full. (Prepare the forms by greasing them and sprinkling the insides with flour. Place on the bottom of the forms round circles of greased paper, the size of the forms. Be sure that both sides of the circles are thoroughly greased.) Set the forms in a warm place and let the dough rise once more (for the third time).

When the dough rises to 3/4 height of the forms, brush the tops of koolichy with egg yolk slightly beaten with a little sugar and place in a pre-heated oven (350°) for 50-60 minutes or until ready. Test the readiness of your koolichy by sticking a toothpick in several places: if the toothpick comes out dry and clean, your koolichy are ready.

If you notice while baking that the koolich is rising up unevenly, turn the form very, very carefully, once, or several times.

If the koolich is in danger of burning, although not yet baked through, place a circle of damp paper over it and reduce heat. Some of the old ovens seem to be very temperamental, so vary the heat of your oven according to your experience with your particular oven.

BABA AU RUM (ROMOVAYA BABA)

Some people insist that Baba au Rum is a French creation. But the majority of Russians claim that this exotic dish is thoroughly Russian, pointing to its name—Baba, which in peasant-Russian means Woman.

Whatever is the origin of this juicy, delectable dessert, I am sure you will enjoy trying this recipe.

1 1/2 pounds sifted white flour	*1 1/2 cups sugar*
	1 1/2 ounces yeast
2 1/2 cups warm milk	*1/2 teaspoon salt*
7 eggs	*1 teaspoon vanilla*
3/4 pound butter or margarine, creamed until white	

SYRUP FOR THE BABA

2/3 cup sugar	*2 cups water*
4-6 tablespoons grape wine or liquor or 1 teaspoon rum extract	

Dissolve yeast in 1 1/4 cups of warm milk. Add half of the flour and mix into a rather thick dough. Roll the dough into a ball, make several cuts in it and place in a pot with warm water (about 3 quarts), cover with a lid, and put in a warm place to rise.

In about 40-50 minutes the dough will rise to the top of the water and will double in size. Take it out of the water and place in a large mixing bowl. Have ready the rest of the warm milk, egg yolks, beaten with sugar until almost white, egg whites, beaten with salt until very stiff, and the rest of the flour. Have the butter or margarine creamed until white. Combine all the ingredients, adding flour bit by bit and mixing the dough until there are no lumps. The dough mustn't be too thick, so add a little more warm milk if necessary.

Put the dough in a warm place to rise and when it doubles in size, place the dough in the forms greased and sprinkled with flour. Let the dough rise once more (in the forms) and when it reaches about 3/4 the height of the form, place the forms in a slow oven (275°-300°) for 45-60 minutes.

While baking, you'll have to turn the forms once or twice, but take the utmost care in doing it, for even the slightest shake might cause the center of the babas to fall and make a hole inside.

When the babas are ready (you test their readiness the same as with koolich), let them cool a little in their forms.

Meanwhile, prepare the syrup:

Dissolve sugar in warm water, add wine or liquor or rum extract and mix thoroughly.

When the babas are cool, take them out of the forms, place on a platter and carefully pour the syrup over them, turning them over to allow for better penetration of the syrup. Collect the drippings of the syrup, warm them up if necessary, and pour over the babas once again. When all the syrup is completely absorbed, place the babas on a serving platter, and serve.

You may store some babas in your refrigerator for later use. In such case, do not pour any syrup over them until they are to be served. If the babas have been stored for a few days, use hot syrup and then cool the babas.

DESSERTS

You'll never hear a Russian say *nyet* to an offer of a dessert. Never! And, in spite of our national sweet tooth, the Russians, as a nation, have surprisingly good teeth! In my whole life in Russia I never saw a child wearing braces, and I myself never had a cavity until I was eighteen years old. Here, in America, I still find it hard to say no to a dessert, but I do —slave that I am to my figure.

But once in a while I indulge myself in all kinds of delicious, gooie things which the waiters in famous restaurants like Romanoff's or the Brown Derby or Perrino's—to mention just a few in my neighborhood—serve from small fancy carts. Oh, to partake of those desserts!

In this book I have tried to compile the most famous Russian desserts. Some of these were adopted by Russians from the French or other nations and are now sincerely considered by the Russians as *Russian* desserts. Others are really Russian. Whichever is the case, they all are delicious and some of them may surprise you when you learn about the ingredients (like farina or cream of wheat in Cranberry Mousse).

Russians like fruit and berry desserts which, unlike in America, are usually strictly seasonal dishes.

On the other hand, Russians eat lots of baked desserts, like sweet pirozhki or pirogi, all kinds of baked things filled with preserves or sweetened cottage cheese.

Some Russian desserts are so filling that I would advise serving them as a sweet luncheon meal, complete in itself, unless, of course, you are serving Russian guests. In such case, don't hesitate to serve it as a dessert even if it is very filling. Your Russian guests will love you for this! I am referring of course to the gurievskaya kasha, one of the most Russian among the Russian desserts.

A few secrets concerning preparation of Russian desserts:

1. Cranberry or Lingonberry Mousse should be eaten the day it is made. Although the taste of the Mousse doesn't change over night, its appearance does. It "falls," and some juice is apt to come out of it.

2. The same applies to any so-called "air-pies," or what we call vozdooshny pirog. It has to be served hot and eaten at once.

3. To have any molded dessert come out of the mold easily, rinse the molds with cold water before filling with the dessert.

4. Always save egg whites. They keep very well for several days in the refrigerator and they can be used on

a minute's notice for making emergency vozdooshny pirog.

5. Gurievskaya kasha may be served cold if you have some of it left over. In such case, have the fruit syrup hot and pour it over the kasha just before serving.

6. Always add a tiny dash of salt to all your sweet dishes.

7. Almond tort keeps for a very long time. But watch out for the cream topping. That won't keep. Actually, don't worry, the chances are that your guests will eat it all!

Most of my recipes require the use of butter. As I have explained in another chapter, this is because I've tried to give you the true Russian recipes, which require butter. The only reason Russians use so much pure butter is that the Russians never had any other shortening good enough to compete with butter. Here, in America, we have all kinds of wonderful shortenings and margarines, so it would be perfectly all right to substitute them for butter if you prefer. However, I still use butter in my own cooking. But this is the way I'm used to cooking.

COTTAGE-CHEESE KOTLETY (TVOROZHNIKY)

1 pound dry cottage cheese (Hoop type)	3-4 tablespoons flour
2 eggs, well beaten	Dash of salt
1 1/2 tablespoons sugar	Cinnamon
2-3 tablespoons sour cream	Sour cream for serving over tvorozhniky
1 teaspoon lemon juice	
1 teaspoon lemon rind, grated	

Use only very dry cottage cheese. (See p. 182 top.) Put cheese through a fine sieve, add sugar, well-beaten eggs, sour cream, lemon juice and lemon rind. Mix very thoroughly. Add salt. Add flour by teaspoonfuls, mixing the mass constantly. Mixture should be very smooth and rather thick. Place in the refrigerator for 45-60 minutes and then scoop small balls of it into a slightly floured board. Form into round or oval kotlety about 3/4 inch thick and about 2-2 1/2 inches in diameter. Fry on both sides in pre-heated butter and serve at once, sprinkled with mixture of cinnamon and sugar and heavy sour cream on the side.

You may also serve tvorozhniky with hot or cold vanilla sauce or with your favorite fruit sauce.

Tvorozhniky could be served also as a main luncheon dish, with a little fruit salad on the side. Serves four.

SHARLOTKA

There is a classic puzzle familiar to every school child. How is one to divide five apples among six children? The answer is simple. Make an apple sauce (or apple pie, as some people tell it).

In Russia we have a slight variation in our answer to the same question: we make sharlotka.

It is a very tasty and inexpensive dessert and quite often it can even be made a one-dish luncheon meal, together with a glass of milk or a cup of coffee.

We Russians prefer our sharlotka made of dark bread. I have tried making it with white bread and it tastes very good also, but still no comparison to the real sharlotka, made with dark bread! I am giving here the two versions of this economical dish.

1 loaf dark bread, without
  crust and preferably stale
6-8 tart apples, minced
1/2 cup butter
1/2 cup sugar
1/2 cup red wine or slightly
  sweetened water

1 teaspoon lemon juice
1/2 teaspoon vanilla
1 teaspoon grated orange
  rind
Cinnamon
Dash of salt

Crumble the bread into tiny pieces and fry them slightly in butter. Remove from heat, add wine or sweetened water, lemon juice, sugar and orange rind. Mix well. Add vanilla.

Grease a mold and sprinkle lightly with bread crumbs.

Place dark bread mixture alternately with minced apples in the mold, sprinkling cinnamon over each layer of apples. The first and the last layer should be bread mixture.

Bake in a slow oven (275°-300°) for 50-60 minutes. Remove from the mold while still hot and serve at once.

You may serve it with any fruit sauce or with plain sweet cream. Or serve it just as it is. Serves four to six people.

SHARLOTKA WITH WHITE BREAD

1 loaf white stale bread,
  without crust
6-8 tart apples, peeled, cored
  and chopped
1/4 pound butter
1 cup sugar

Cinnamon
1 teaspoon vanilla
1 cup water
Bread crumbs
Dash of salt

Crumble the bread and fry it quickly in butter. Combine sugar, vanilla and salt with water and bring to a quick boil. Add apples and cook for 5-10 minutes. Grease a baking dish and sprinkle the inside of it with bread crumbs. Place a layer of bread, alternating it with a layer of apple mixture, sprinkling cinnamon over each apple layer.

The last layer should be bread again. Sprinkle the top with sugar and bake in a slow oven (300°) until golden brown. If sharlotka begins to burn, cover the top with a double layer of waxed paper.

Serve with your favorite fruit sauce, or plain.

Serves four to six people.

GURIEVSKAYA KASHA I

Gurievskaya kasha is the pièce de résistance of Russian desserts. It is a rather heavy pudding, filled with fruits and nuts and served hot. For those who have a sweet tooth, gurievskaya kasha could well serve as a one-dish meal, made complete with a little coffee or a glass of milk on the side.

1/2 pound shelled pecans or walnuts

3 cups milk {*or 6 cups of*
3 cups cream {*"half & half"*

3/4 cup of farina, semolina or cream of wheat

1/2 cup sugar

1 cup mixed candied fruit (or 1 cup chopped and drained canned fruit)

1/2 cup seedless raisins, chopped very fine

1/2 teaspoon vanilla extract

1/2 teaspoon almond extract

1 teaspoon cinnamon

Bread crumbs, sifted several times

Powdered sugar, sifted several times, just enough to sprinkle the top

Blanch the pecans (or walnuts) in boiling water. Remove the skins. Put the nuts through a grinder.

Combine milk and cream and bring to a boil. Add semolina (or farina or cream of wheat) very slowly, stirring constantly. Cook for 6-8 minutes or until kasha thickens. Remove from the fire and add raisins, ground nuts, sugar, and vanilla and almond extracts, mixing thoroughly.

Grease a baking dish and put in it a layer of cooked kasha. Spread over it a thin layer of candied or canned fruits. Then another layer of kasha and again a layer of fruits or some fruit preserve and so on. The top layer should be kasha again.

Sprinkle the very top with sifted bread crumbs, cinnamon and powdered sugar. Brown kasha in a very hot oven or under a broiler, but watch that it doesn't burn. Let cool for 15-20 minutes (usually it cools off sufficiently while you're eating your dinner and is ready to be served at dessert time).

Serve it warm, directly from the baking dish. You may serve it with some fruit syrup or with sweetened red wine, poured over individual servings. Serves six people.

There is another, more complicated way of preparing this dessert. Purists of the Russian cuisine insist that the second way is the one and only way of preparing gurievskaya kasha. If you insist on complete authenticity of your gurievskaya kasha, by all means, use only the second method!

II. Gurievskaya Kasha

Use the same amounts and the same ingredients as in the first recipe, but follow the next procedure:

Blanch the nuts in the boiling water. Remove the skins. Put the nuts through a grinder. Combine milk and cream (in this case do not use "half and half") in a wide enameled pan. Heat VERY slowly. As soon as a golden skin forms on the top of the milk, scoop it off very carefully and put it aside on a large platter. Repeat the process several times. When you have 4-5 skimmed rings on your platter (make sure that the skins don't stick to one another), bring the liquid to a quick boil. Add semolina or farina or cream of wheat very slowly, stirring constantly. Cook for 6-8 minutes. Remove from the fire and add raisins, nuts, sugar, vanilla and almond extracts. Grease a baking dish and put in it a layer of prepared kasha. Over it put one of the milk skins and spread over it a thin layer of candied fruits. Then again a layer of kasha and a milk skin. Repeat the process until all the ingredients are gone, however the top layer should be kasha. Sprinkle the top with bread crumbs, mixed with the powdered sugar and cinnamon and brown kasha in a very hot oven or directly under a broiler. Take care not to burn it. Serve warm, right from the baking dish. You may serve it with some fruit syrup, or with some sweetened red wine, poured over individual servings. Serves six people.

III. GURIEVSKAYA KASHA

For those who don't like the slow method of preparing gurievskaya kasha by skimming milk several times, there is another, quicker, but equally delicious recipe.

1/2 cup farina or semolina or cream of wheat	2 slices canned pineapple
1/2 cup sugar	2 halves canned pears
1/2 cup seedless raisins	4-6 halves canned apricots
2-3 egg yolks (depending on the size of eggs)	6-8 Maraschino cherries
	3-4 halves canned peaches
4 cups milk	1 teaspoon vanilla
	Dash of salt

Combine milk, vanilla and salt and bring to a boil. Slowly add farina or semolina or cream of wheat, stirring constantly, and cook over a low flame until the mixture thickens. Beat egg yolks with sugar until very light and beat farina or semolina or cream of wheat into the egg mixture. Add raisins and cook over very low fire for 2-4 more minutes. Grease and sprinkle with sugar a mold and fill it with prepared kasha. Bake in a hot oven (475°-500°) for just a few minutes, to melt and caramelize the sugar.

Remove kasha from the mold, place on a shallow baking dish or a platter (or on a pie tin) and decorate the top and the sides of kasha with canned fruits, thoroughly drained. Sprinkle generously with sugar all over and place under a broiler for a few minutes. Watch that the kasha doesn't burn.

Just before serving, if you like the flavor of kirsch, you may sprinkle it over the kasha and set it aflame. But this has been mainly an American innovation.

Serve with apricot or cherry sauce (1/2 cup apricot or cherry preserve mixed with 1/2 cup warm water and 1 tablespoon rum or any liqueur). Serve hot. Serves four to six.

TRADITIONAL EASTER DESSERT (PASKHA)

2 1/2 pounds dry cottage cheese (the cottage cheese must be very dry)
5 large eggs
1/2 pound melted butter
1 pound sugar
1/2 pint sour cream

1 teaspoon vanilla
1/2 pound almonds, blanched and shredded
1/2 cup candied orange or lemon peel or mixture of both
1/2 cup seedless raisins

The main secret in making really good paskha is to have very dry cottage cheese. Don't even attempt to make paskha unless you are able to get really dry cottage cheese, the kind that hasn't been creamed. I have tried several times to make paskha with creamed cottage cheese and each time it was a complete failure. Finally, someone recommended that I try so-called Hoop Cottage Cheese, which is sold packed like any creamed cheese. This cheese is very dry and it makes an excellent paskha.

Crumble the cheese (if you are using the commercial pre-packed Hoop cheese) and force it through a coarse sieve twice.

Beat egg yolks with sugar until very light. Add vanilla and sour cream. Slowly add melted butter; continue to beat until all the ingredients are completely mixed. Combine the cottage cheese with the egg yolk mixture. Beat the egg whites with a dash of salt until stiff. Fold carefully into cottage cheese and mix thoroughly. Add almonds, raisins and candied orange or lemon peel.

Cook on a very slow fire until the bubbles form at the edges of the kettle. Remove from fire and chill in the same kettle.

When cool, pour the mixture into a colander, lined with cheesecloth or a napkin, and let it drip for 2-3 hours.

Without removing the cheesecloth or the napkin, place the mixture in a conical form (a large, unglazed, clay flower pot served me beautifully for, like the majority of American women, I don't have the traditional Russian paskha form).

Place a small saucer over the folded ends of the cheesecloth or napkin, put a weight over it and let the excess of moisture come out through the draining hole of the flower pot. To make sure that the moisture drips freely, place the flower pot in such a way that its bottom doesn't touch the drippings below it.

Put the whole contraption in the refrigerator for several hours (I usually leave it there overnight).

Just before serving paskha, remove the weights, unfold the edges of the cheesecloth or napkin, place a large plate or platter over the flower pot and turn it over very carefully. Remove the cheesecloth with the utmost care, for the paskha might break.

Decorate the very top with an artificial flower (it looks naive, but it is traditional!).

Slice horizontally and serve with koolich. Paskha will keep for a long time in the refrigerator, but cover it tightly with waxed paper to prevent drying out.

Serves six to ten people.

FRUIT DESSERT (KISEL)

The most famous of Russian kisels is the cranberry kisel. Russian cranberries are smaller than their American counterparts. They have thinner skins, they are juicier and more sour. They grow wild in the marshes of northern Russia and gathering them was one of the exciting experiences of my childhood. There was always an element of danger attached to such expeditions, for some of the marshes were bottomless pits, where a man could lose his life in quicksand.

The closest I have come to finding Russian-type cranberries in the U.S. was when I stumbled on lingonberries; however, it is not imperative that you use lingonberries. If you can't get them, use fine, ripe cranberries.

A must in preparing any Russian kisel is having the right kind of starch. My Russian friends insist that only potato starch will do. Well, I have tried traditional American cornstarch and I find nothing wrong with it. But, of course, you cannot argue with a Russian when it comes to such a sacred thing as kisel!

So, try to use potato starch if you can, but in case you can't get it—use cornstarch. The result, in both cases is very rewarding.

1 1/2 pounds cranberries or
    lingonberries
1 1/4 cups sugar
1 tablespoon potato starch or
    cornstarch for each 2 cups
    of liquid

Dash of salt
Cream or milk to serve on
    the side

Wash and sort the berries, using only the perfect ones. Place them in a pot and cover with just enough water to cover the top of the berries. Simmer slowly for 10-12 minutes. Put the berries and juice through a sieve. Add sugar and bring to a boil.

Measure the mixture. Use one tablespoon of potato or cornstarch for each two cups of mixture. Dissolve the starch in a small amount of cold water. When completely dissolved, add one cup of berry mixture and mix well. Blend the starch mixture with the berry mixture and once more bring to a boil. Remove from fire and ladle into individual serving dishes. Cool thoroughly for several hours and serve with cold milk or cream on the side. Keeps very well in the refrigerator for several days. Serves four to six people.

BLUEBERRY KISEL

1 1/2 pounds blueberries
1 1/4 cups sugar
2 teaspoons grated lemon
rind

Potato starch or cornstarch
(1 tablespoon of starch for
each 2 cups of liquid)

Prepare the berries by using only the perfect ones. Add just enough water to cover them and cook over a slow fire for 10-15 minutes.

Force the berries and the juice through a fine sieve and add sugar and lemon rind. Bring to a quick boil. Measure the mixture and use one tablespoon of starch for two cups of liquid. Dissolve the starch in a small amount of cold water, then add one cup of the berry juice. Mix well and combine with the rest of the berry mixture. Bring to a boil again and remove from the fire. Pour into individual serving dishes and chill for a few hours. Serve with cold milk or cream.

This kisel is particularly beneficial to convalescing persons and to children recuperating from upset stomachs. It is very light and yet it is binding. Serves four to six.

KISEL MADE OF DRIED FRUITS

1/2 pound dried fruits—apri-
cots or peaches or prunes
or mixture of all
1/2 cup sugar (or more if the
fruits are very dry)

1 tablespoon of starch for
each 2 cups of liquid

Soak the dry fruits in just enough cold water to cover their tops. Let stand for 2-3 hours. Drain the fruits and measure the remaining liquid. Add just enough water to have 6 cups of liquid.

Combine the fruit with the liquid and bring to a boil. Reduce heat and cook slowly until the fruit is completely tender. Force through a sieve. Add sugar. Dissolve potato or cornstarch in a small amount of cold water and add one cup of the fruit liquid. Mix well. Combine with the rest of fruit mixture. If you want a thicker kisel, use a little more starch.

Bring to a boil once more and remove from heat. Pour into individual serving dishes, cool for 2-3 hours and serve with heavy cream or plain cold milk. Serves four to six people.

Kisel Made of Apples (Yablochny Kisel)

1 1/4 pounds peeled and
　　cored apples
1 cup sugar

2 1/2 cups water
1 1/2 tablespoons potato or
　　cornstarch

Slice peeled and cored apples, add water and cook until the apples are completely soft. Drain the apples and measure the liquid. Dissolve starch in a small amount of cold water and add one cup of apple stock. Mix thoroughly.

Add sugar and apple pulp to the remaining apple stock and bring to a boil. While boiling, slowly but steadily add the starch mixture.

Slowly boil for 2-3 minutes. Remove from fire, pour into individual serving dishes and cool thoroughly. Serves four to six people.

KISEL MADE OF FRESH CHERRIES (VISHNEVY KISEL)

2 1/2 cups cherries (measure   1 1/2 cups sugar
   the cherries after you   4 1/2 cups hot water
   have taken out the   3-4 tablespoons potato or
   pits)   cornstarch

Combine pitted cherries with sugar and let stand for 1/2 hour. Stir the cherries during this time several times to accumulate as much cherry juice as possible. Drain the cherries and save the juice.

Crush the cherry pits in a mortar until very fine and pour 1 1/2 cups of boiling water over them. Let stand for 10 minutes and then boil for another 5-7 minutes. Strain twice and pour over the cherry and sugar mixture. Bring to a boil.

Dissolve starch in a small amount of cold water, then add one cup of hot water and mix thoroughly. Add starch mixture to a boiling fruit mixture, stirring constantly. Add the cherry juice and stir.

Pour into individual serving dishes and chill thoroughly. Serve with cold milk or cream. Serves four to eight people.

KISEL MADE WITH MILK (MOLOCHNY KISEL)

4 1/2 cups milk   4-5 drops of almond extract
3/4 cup sugar   1 teaspoon vanilla
2 tablespoons potato or cornstarch

Boil 3 cups of milk and add sugar. Dissolve starch in 1/2 cup of cold milk and add the remaining one cup of milk. Mix well. Slowly add to the hot milk and cook for 5 minutes on a very slow fire, stirring constantly. Remove from fire and add vanilla and almond extract. While still hot, pour into individual serving dishes and cool thoroughly. Just before serving you may turn the dishes upside down and have individual little molds, or you may serve molochny kisel in the serving dishes. Serves six to eight people.

COMPOTE MADE OF DRIED FRUITS

In Russia, where the fresh fruits are to be had only in season, dry fruits have an enormous popularity. Russians usually like their dried fruits mixed—the more varied the combination, the better.

1/2 pound mixed dried fruits   *4 1/2 cups water*
   (a few prunes, apricots,   *3/4 cup sugar*
   raisins, dried apples,
   dates, dried pears,
   peaches, etc.)

Wash dry fruits in warm water and sort out the apples and pears. Place the apples and pears in a pot and add water. Cook very slowly for 25-30 minutes. Add the remaining fruits and sugar and cook for 5-10 minutes more. Remove from fire, and cool. Serve from an attractive tureen, at the table. Serves six to eight people.

RED WINE JELLY

1 1/4 cups red wine   *1 teaspoon lemon juice*
1 cup sugar   *1 teaspoon vanilla*
2 1/2 cups hot water
4 packs of unflavored gela-
   tine

Dissolve gelatine in one cup of cold water.

Place sugar and hot water in a pot and, stirring briskly, add dissolved gelatine. Bring to a boil. Add wine, lemon juice and vanilla. Strain the mixture, cool slightly and pour into individual forms. Cool thoroughly and remove from forms just before serving.

You may decorate each serving with frozen or fresh fruits. Serves six to eight people.

CRANBERRY OR LINGONBERRY MOUSSE

Ever since I was a child I have loved Cranberry Mousse. Unfortunately, it was only on rare occasions that I was able to indulge in this inexpensive but tasty dessert.

The trouble was the beating. The mousse required a lot of beating! And my grandmother detested long beating by hand.

When I grew up and started cooking, I too found that with all my yen for cranberry mousse, I just couldn't face hours of beating! Fortunately, the problem doesn't exist here in America where we have electric beaters or, at least, rotary beaters, and thus we can make this dessert within minutes. Try it, I am sure you will like its fresh flavor and attractive appearance.

1 1/4 cups cranberries or lingonberries
1 1/4 cups sugar

3 3/4 cups water
3 tablespoons cream of wheat or farina or semolina

Place washed and sorted berries in a sack or cheesecloth, folded several times. Put in a pot and squash thoroughly. Add one cup lukewarm water and squeeze all the liquid out. Place the resulting juice in the refrigerator for further use.

Add the remaining water to the berries' pulp and boil for 5 minutes. Strain the liquid thoroughly (more than once if necessary) and throw away the pulp.

Put the liquid back on a slow fire and add cream of wheat very slowly, while the liquid continues to boil. Stirring constantly, boil slowly for 15-20 minutes, then add sugar, bring to a boil again and take off the fire. Add the juice from the first squeezing of the berries and beat constantly until the mousse doubles in size.

Ladle into individual serving dishes and place in the refrigerator. Serve when absolutely cool. You may serve the mousse with cold milk on the side.

The mousse could be prepared from almost any kind of berries. Use your own imagination and the same basic proportions. Serves six to eight people.

HONEY MOUSSE

Honey is one of the most popular of Russian cooking ingredients. For generations Russian peasants used natural wild honey as a sweetening in all cooking, sugar being either completely unknown to them or too expensive to use in everyday life.

Here is a delicious honey dessert, which looks and tastes very good and is bound to be a favorite with children.

1 1/4 cups honey
4 eggs, separated

1 cup whipped cream (optional, to use instead of egg whites)

Separate the eggs. Beat the yolks and add honey very gradually.

As soon as the egg yolks and honey are completely mixed, cook them over a very slow fire, stirring constantly, until the mass thickens. Remove from fire and cool.

Beat the egg whites until stiff and combine with the honey mixture. Mix thoroughly. Place the mousse in serving dishes and chill.

You may use whipped cream, beaten very stiff, in place of the egg whites. Serves four to six people.

STUFFED BAKED APPLES

6 large tart apples	*1/3 cup sugar*
1/4 cup seedless raisins	*1 egg*
1/4 cup shredded almonds	*2 tablespoons butter*
1/3 cup cooked rice (prefera-	*Syrup—raspberry or black*
bly cooked in milk)	*currant*

Core the apples and carefully remove part of the apples' meat, making sure that the outside of the apples remains without any cuts.

Combine raisins, almonds, rice. Add melted butter. Slightly beat egg with sugar and combine with the rest of the ingredients. Fill the centers of the apples with the stuffing and place the apples in a baking dish. Add 6 tablespoons of boiling water and bake in a moderate oven (375°) until tender, basting with the syrup from the bottom of the baking dish. As soon as the apples are ready, place them on a serving platter and cool. Serve with raspberry or black-currant syrup or with any of your favorite preserves. Serves six people and is nourishing enough to be used as a one-dish luncheon meal. In such case, serve two apples for each person.

CRIMEAN CREAM (SOUR CREAM DESSERT)

1 1/3 cups sour cream
2/3 cup powdered sugar
1 pack of unflavored gelatine
1/2 teaspoon vanilla

2/3 cup pulp of strawberries
or raspberries or blue-
berries (optional)

Wash and sort the berries, crush them and force them through a fine sieve. Place sour cream, sugar and vanilla in a bowl and beat with an electric beater (or a rotary beater) until the mixture doubles in size and becomes very fluffy. The sour cream must be very cold so, if necessary, place the bowl in a larger one, filled with ice, and continue to keep the ingredients very cold throughout the mixing process.

Dissolve gelatine in a small amount of warm water and slowly add to the sour-cream mixture, blending it thoroughly. Pour into individual serving dishes or forms and chill for several hours.

If you use the berries, add them to the mixture before you add gelatine. Otherwise, continue the process as described above.

CREAM AU RUM

1 cup cream
2 egg yolks

2 1/2 tablespoons sugar
4-5 tablespoons rum

Have whipping cream very cold.

Beat egg yolks with sugar until very smooth and almost white in color. Slowly add cream, continuing to beat until very fluffy. Gently stir in rum. Serve right away in individual serving dishes.

You may serve this cream over fresh fruits or some not-too-sweet cake (it brightens up a leftover dry cake).

Serves four to six people.

APRICOT CREAM "CRIMEAN DELIGHT"

3/4 cup apricot pulp
1/2 cup whipping cream
1 cup milk
1/3 cup sugar
3 eggs, separated

1/2 teaspoon vanilla
1 teaspoon lemon juice
1 envelope unflavored gelatine

Dissolve gelatine in a small amount of lukewarm water. Beat egg yolks with sugar and slowly add milk, stirring constantly. Cook in a double boiler until the mixture thickens, stirring all the time.

Add gelatine and stir until it is completely dissolved. Cool. Add apricot pulp. (Prepare the fruit by crushing it and forcing it through a fine sieve. Or you may use canned apricots. Force them through a sieve also.) Add vanilla and lemon juice.

Beat the egg whites until very stiff. Beat the whipped cream until very stiff and combine the two.

Fold into the egg-yolk mixture and gently stir.

Place in a mold (or individual molds) and thoroughly chill for several hours.

Serves four to six people.

COFFEE CREAM

1/2 cup very strong coffee
1 1/4 cups whipping cream
3/4 cup powdered sugar

1/2 teaspoon vanilla
1/2 envelope unflavored gelatine

Dissolve gelatine in lukewarm coffee. Have the whipping cream very cold and beat it slowly, adding sugar until quite stiff. Add vanilla and very gradually add gelatine, beating all the time.

Place in a mold (or molds) and chill for a few hours. Serves four to six people.

BAKED APPLES A LA RUSSE

6 large tart apples	*Almonds, blanched and*
1 cup Madeira wine	*shredded*
1/2 cup light brown sugar	*Cream (optional)*
1 teaspoon cinnamon	

Core the apples, making sure that you don't cut too deep, in order to prevent any possible loss of juice. Mix brown sugar with cinnamon and fill the centers of the apples. Place in a baking dish and add 6 tablespoons of boiling water. Bake in a rather hot oven (400°-425°) basting frequently. When the apples are partly done, add wine and continue to bake until completely done. Throughout the baking process baste the apples with the syrup from the bottom of the baking dish.

When the apples are done, sprinkle their tops generously with the almonds and pour over them the remaining syrup.

Cool thoroughly (but do not put them in a refrigerator) and serve with fresh thick cream on the side. Serves six people.

APPLE PIE MADE OF "AIR!" (VOZDUSHNY PIROG)

This is a very attractive dessert, served hot. It is extremely easy to prepare and it is so light that even the most caloryconscious person won't object to have a second helping. The only negative feature of this "airy" dessert is its tendency to fall if not served immediately. But this can easily be avoided by properly planning the preparation of the entire meal and by having the vozdushny pirog in the oven during the 10-15 minutes it takes your family or guests to eat their main course. By proper timing you will be able to avoid the "falling" of the air pie.

3/4 pound apples (tart apples are the best)
6 egg whites
1 1/4 cups sugar
2 tablespoons powdered sugar
1-2 tablespoons water

Core and peel apples and cut them into medium-sized chunks. Place in a baking dish, add water and bake in the moderate oven until soft. Cool. Force through a sieve and add sugar. Cook over a slow fire until the purée becomes thick and stops dripping from the spoon.

Beat the egg whites until very stiff. Slowly add apple purée and mix thoroughly. Place in a baking dish from which you are to serve the pirog and smooth the top with a knife or spatula (have the baking dish slightly greased). Place vozdushny pirog in a moderate oven (375°) for 10-15 minutes or until pirog becomes high and golden. Serve at once from the same dish, sprinkle the top with powdered sugar. Serves four.

You may also make vozdushny pirog with apple sauce or with apple purée put out by various brands, or with any of your favorite preserves. If you use store-bought preserves, watch out for the amount of sugar in the recipe. If the preserves are quite sweet, cut down the amount of sugar, according to your taste.

Actually any fruit can make a wonderful vozdushny pirog, so if you like the general idea, try to experiment and create some new combinations. If you will use any commercial brand preserves or purées, watch out also for the amount of liquid in them. If there is too much liquid, strain the preserves or purées and cook them for a few minutes to make them thicker.

ALMOND TORT

This is a very unusual dessert. Although it is baked like a cake, it doesn't require any flour. Not a dash!

1 pound blanched and	*2 1/2 cups sugar*
shredded almonds	*2/3 cup bread crumbs*
10 eggs	*1/2 tablespoon butter*

FILLING

2 cups heavy cream	*2 tablespoons shredded al-*
1 1/4 cups sugar	*monds, slightly browned in*
1/4 teaspoon vanilla	*the oven*

Put almonds through a meat grinder. Beat eggs with sugar until almost white. Combine with the almonds and stir until thoroughly mixed. Grease with butter and sprinkle with bread crumbs two forms with removable bottoms and bake in moderate oven (350°-375°) for 12-15 minutes.

While you are baking the almond tort, prepare the following filling:

Place cream in an enameled pot, add sugar and vanilla and cook over a slow fire, constantly stirring, until the mixture thickens and begins to change its color toward light brown. Remove from fire and cool. When the cream mixture is cool, beat it for one minute with a rotary-beater or at a slow speed with an electric beater.

When the almond tort parts are done, cool them and remove from the forms. Place one almond tort circle on a serving platter, heap with the cream mixture and cover with the second part of the almond tort. Spread the remaining cream filling over the top and sides of the tort and sprinkle the whole tort with the shredded and browned almonds.

The result—a delicious dessert, which is bound to be also a conversation piece. Serves six.

PIROZHNOYE

Lovers of French pastries will recognize the following recipe and will insist that it is a French pastry recipe. I won't argue. Except that we Russians have always believed it to be a Russian pastry!

Whichever it may be, the recipe for this pirozhnoye is one of the least complicated, and is almost foolproof.

1 1/4 cups sifted flour
1/4 teaspoon salt
1 1/4 cups water

4-5 eggs
1/4 lb unsalted butter or
margarine

Combine water, salt and butter and bring to a boil. Reduce heat and add flour, constantly stirring. Cook for 2-3 minutes, stirring all the time. Remove from the fire and add eggs one at a time, stirring constantly and thoroughly. As soon as the dough begins to stretch, stop adding eggs. Grease a baking sheet very slightly and place the dough on it in the form of little balls or ovals, at 1 1/2 inch intervals.

Preheat the oven to 400° and bake pirozhnoye for 15-20

minutes. As soon as pirozhnoye doubles in size and begins to turn golden, reduce heat to 350° and continue to bake until completely done.

Remove pirozhnoye from the oven and cool. Slice one side of each pirozhnoye and fill the hollows with the following cream:

FILLING

1/2 pound unsalted butter	*1 egg*
1 1/4 cups sugar	*1/4 teaspoon vanilla or 2-3*
2/3 cup milk	*tablespoons liqueur*

Beat sugar and egg until almost white. Add milk and cook slowly, constantly stirring until the mixture starts to boil. Remove from fire and cool. Beat butter until white and fluffy. Add cooled mixture of egg and milk, continuing to beat. Add vanilla or liqueur.

Sprinkle pirozhnoye with powdered sugar and serve. Serves six.

APPLE MOLDS A LA RUM

4 large, tart apples	*3-4 tablespoons cold water*
2 tablespoons rum	*1/2 cup hot water*
1/2 cup sugar	*Juice of 1/2 lemon*
1 cup heavy cream	*Grated rind of 1/2 lemon*
1 pack gelatine	*White of 1 egg*

Core and peel the apples, place them in a baking dish and bake until done. Force the apples through a sieve and cool. Add egg white and beat until very fluffy. Continue to beat at a slower speed while adding sugar. As soon as all the sugar is absorbed, beat at a faster speed until the mixture is stiff. Have gelatine dissolved in cold water, then add hot water, constantly stirring. As soon as the gelatine begins to thicken again, combine it with the apple mixture. Add rum, lemon juice and lemon rind. Beat cream until very stiff and combine with the apple mixture.

Rinse a mold (or individual molds) with cold water and without drying the insides of the mold, pour the apple mixture into it. Chill thoroughly for several hours (or overnight) and unmold before serving by quickly wiping the sides of the mold with a hot, wet towel.

Serves four to six people.

LITTLE SECRETS GATHERED AT RANDOM

If you want to clear a cloudy-looking lemon juice, add 2-3 tablespoons of fresh milk. The milk will curdle and it will clear the juice.

Coring apples—never peel the apples before coring. They might fall apart.

Don't dispose of the cores and the apple peels. Collect them and boil them in 2 1/2 cups of water together with one cup of sugar. Strain thoroughly and give to the children to relieve an irritating tickle in the throat. This is not a medicine, but just a pleasant-tasting, harmless syrup, which usually helps to stop a light cough.

The same idea can apply to any fruit waste, so don't *waste* it! Forgive me the pun.

While browning flour in butter, always have butter (or other shortening) sizzling hot. It prevents flour from becoming soggy.

The best kind of soup greens for consommés and other clear soups, are old, large, full-grown vegetables. The younger vegetables cook much faster and lose much of their flavor during the long process of clear-soup making. Have these old pieces of vegetables sliced lengthwise and brown them quickly in butter, or any other shortening. Or, if you have a griddle, place them cut-side down on the griddle and let them burn slightly. Watch that they are only *slightly* burned!

Never cover *pirog* or *pirozhky* to keep them warm. The

cover will make their crusts soggy, so, if you want to keep your pirog or pirozhky hot, place them in a warm oven with the door wide open. Don't overdo it, for you might dry them out if you keep them in the oven too long.

Be careful in adding seasoning to foods containing spicy ingredients, like bacon, dill pickles, sauerkraut and so forth. Always taste the food before adding any seasoning and even then, add it only in small amounts.

In some fresh-vegetable salads, which need a "hint" of garlic, give it with a small piece of pumpernickel crust, rubbed with raw garlic. Place this piece of pumpernickel crust at the bottom of your salad, and remove it just before serving.

Serve wedges of lemon with any kind of fish. Lemon not only gives fish a special, more delicate flavor, but it also takes away the taste of fish if there is another dish to be served after the fish.

Rinse the uncut lemon with boiling water just before slicing, before serving the lemon wedges, to give a stronger aroma.

Never use new potatoes for making mashed potatoes. Use older potatoes, for they are meatier. On the other hand, use new potatoes for salads and whenever the potatoes are to be served whole, as a side dish to the entrée.

In cooking fresh vegetables, never allow the water to evaporate. Always keep the pot tightly covered. Cook the vegetables in salted water; it locks in the juices of the vegetables during the cooking process.

To distinguish between cooked and raw egg without breaking the shell, spin the egg. The cooked egg will spin several times before stopping, while the raw egg will make only one or two turns.

Index

203

A CATALOG OF SELECTED
DOVER BOOKS
IN ALL FIELDS OF INTEREST

A CATALOG OF SELECTED DOVER
BOOKS IN ALL FIELDS OF INTEREST

CONCERNING THE SPIRITUAL IN ART, Wassily Kandinsky. Pioneering work by father of abstract art. Thoughts on color theory, nature of art. Analysis of earlier masters. 12 illustrations. 80pp. of text. 5⅜ x 8½.　　23411-8 Pa. $4.95

ANIMALS: 1,419 Copyright-Free Illustrations of Mammals, Birds, Fish, Insects, etc., Jim Harter (ed.). Clear wood engravings present, in extremely lifelike poses, over 1,000 species of animals. One of the most extensive pictorial sourcebooks of its kind. Captions. Index. 284pp. 9 x 12.　　23766-4 Pa. $14.95

CELTIC ART: The Methods of Construction, George Bain. Simple geometric techniques for making Celtic interlacements, spirals, Kells-type initials, animals, humans, etc. Over 500 illustrations. 160pp. 9 x 12. (USO)　　22923-8 Pa. $9.95

AN ATLAS OF ANATOMY FOR ARTISTS, Fritz Schider. Most thorough reference work on art anatomy in the world. Hundreds of illustrations, including selections from works by Vesalius, Leonardo, Goya, Ingres, Michelangelo, others. 593 illustrations. 192pp. 7⅛ x 10¼.　　20241-0 Pa. $9.95

CELTIC HAND STROKE-BY-STROKE (Irish Half-Uncial from "The Book of Kells"): An Arthur Baker Calligraphy Manual, Arthur Baker. Complete guide to creating each letter of the alphabet in distinctive Celtic manner. Covers hand position, strokes, pens, inks, paper, more. Illustrated. 48pp. 8¼ x 11.　　24336-2 Pa. $3.95

EASY ORIGAMI, John Montroll. Charming collection of 32 projects (hat, cup, pelican, piano, swan, many more) specially designed for the novice origami hobbyist. Clearly illustrated easy-to-follow instructions insure that even beginning papercrafters will achieve successful results. 48pp. 8¼ x 11.　　27298-2 Pa. $3.50

THE COMPLETE BOOK OF BIRDHOUSE CONSTRUCTION FOR WOODWORKERS, Scott D. Campbell. Detailed instructions, illustrations, tables. Also data on bird habitat and instinct patterns. Bibliography. 3 tables. 63 illustrations in 15 figures. 48pp. 5¼ x 8½.　　24407-5 Pa. $2.50

BLOOMINGDALE'S ILLUSTRATED 1886 CATALOG: Fashions, Dry Goods and Housewares, Bloomingdale Brothers. Famed merchants' extremely rare catalog depicting about 1,700 products: clothing, housewares, firearms, dry goods, jewelry, more. Invaluable for dating, identifying vintage items. Also, copyright-free graphics for artists, designers. Co-published with Henry Ford Museum & Greenfield Village. 160pp. 8¼ x 11.　　25780-0 Pa. $10.95

HISTORIC COSTUME IN PICTURES, Braun & Schneider. Over 1,450 costumed figures in clearly detailed engravings–from dawn of civilization to end of 19th century. Captions. Many folk costumes. 256pp. 8⅜ x 11¾.　　23150-X Pa. $12.95

STICKLEY CRAFTSMAN FURNITURE CATALOGS, Gustav Stickley and L. & J. G. Stickley. Beautiful, functional furniture in two authentic catalogs from 1910. 594 illustrations, including 277 photos, show settles, rockers, armchairs, reclining chairs, bookcases, desks, tables. 183pp. 6½ x 9¼. 23838-5 Pa. $11.95

AMERICAN LOCOMOTIVES IN HISTORIC PHOTOGRAPHS: 1858 to 1949, Ron Ziel (ed.). A rare collection of 126 meticulously detailed official photographs, called "builder portraits," of American locomotives that majestically chronicle the rise of steam locomotive power in America. Introduction. Detailed captions. xi + 129pp. 9 x 12. 27393-8 Pa. $13.95

AMERICA'S LIGHTHOUSES: An Illustrated History, Francis Ross Holland, Jr. Delightfully written, profusely illustrated fact-filled survey of over 200 American light-houses since 1716. History, anecdotes, technological advances, more. 240pp. 8 x 10¾. 25576-X Pa. $12.95

TOWARDS A NEW ARCHITECTURE, Le Corbusier. Pioneering manifesto by founder of "International School." Technical and aesthetic theories, views of indus-try, economics, relation of form to function, "mass-production split" and much more. Profusely illustrated. 320pp. 6⅛ x 9¼. (USO) 25023-7 Pa. $9.95

HOW THE OTHER HALF LIVES, Jacob Riis. Famous journalistic record, expos-ing poverty and degradation of New York slums around 1900, by major social reformer. 100 striking and influential photographs. 233pp. 10 x 7⅞. 22012-5 Pa. $11.95

FRUIT KEY AND TWIG KEY TO TREES AND SHRUBS, William M. Harlow. One of the handiest and most widely used identification aids. Fruit key covers 120 deciduous and evergreen species; twig key 160 deciduous species. Easily used. Over 300 photographs. 126pp. 5⅜ x 8½. 20511-8 Pa. $3.95

COMMON BIRD SONGS, Dr. Donald J. Borror. Songs of 60 most common U.S. birds: robins, sparrows, cardinals, bluejays, finches, more–arranged in order of increasing complexity. Up to 9 variations of songs of each species. Cassette and manual 99911-4 $8.95

ORCHIDS AS HOUSE PLANTS, Rebecca Tyson Northen. Grow cattleyas and many other kinds of orchids–in a window, in a case, or under artificial light. 63 illus-trations. 148pp. 5⅜ x 8½. 23261-1 Pa. $5.95

MONSTER MAZES, Dave Phillips. Masterful mazes at four levels of difficulty. Avoid deadly perils and evil creatures to find magical treasures. Solutions for all 32 exciting illustrated puzzles. 48pp. 8¼ x 11. 26005-4 Pa. $2.95

MOZART'S DON GIOVANNI (DOVER OPERA LIBRETTO SERIES), Wolfgang Amadeus Mozart. Introduced and translated by Ellen H. Bleiler. Standard Italian libretto, with complete English translation. Convenient and thoroughly portable–an ideal companion for reading along with a recording or the performance itself. Introduction. List of characters. Plot summary. 121pp. 5¼ x 8½. 24944-1 Pa. $3.95

TECHNICAL MANUAL AND DICTIONARY OF CLASSICAL BALLET, Gail Grant. Defines, explains, comments on steps, movements, poses and concepts. 15-page pictorial section. Basic book for student, viewer. 127pp. 5⅜ x 8½. 21843-0 Pa. $4.95

THE CLARINET AND CLARINET PLAYING, David Pino. Lively, comprehensive work features suggestions about technique, musicianship, and musical interpretation, as well as guidelines for teaching, making your own reeds, and preparing for public performance. Includes an intriguing look at clarinet history. "A godsend," The Clarinet, Journal of the International Clarinet Society. Appendixes. 7 illus. 320pp. 5⅜ x 8½. 40270-3 Pa. $9.95

HOLLYWOOD GLAMOR PORTRAITS, John Kobal (ed.). 145 photos from 1926-49. Harlow, Gable, Bogart, Bacall; 94 stars in all. Full background on photographers, technical aspects. 160pp. 8⅜ x 11¼. 23352-9 Pa. $12.95

THE ANNOTATED CASEY AT THE BAT: A Collection of Ballads about the Mighty Casey/Third, Revised Edition, Martin Gardner (ed.). Amusing sequels and parodies of one of America's best-loved poems: Casey's Revenge, Why Casey Whiffed, Casey's Sister at the Bat, others. 256pp. 5⅜ x 8½. 28598-7 Pa. $8.95

THE RAVEN AND OTHER FAVORITE POEMS, Edgar Allan Poe. Over 40 of the author's most memorable poems: "The Bells," "Ulalume," "Israfel," "To Helen," "The Conqueror Worm," "Eldorado," "Annabel Lee," many more. Alphabetic lists of titles and first lines. 64pp. 5³⁄₁₆ x 8¼. 26685-0 Pa. $1.00

PERSONAL MEMOIRS OF U. S. GRANT, Ulysses Simpson Grant. Intelligent, deeply moving firsthand account of Civil War campaigns, considered by many the finest military memoirs ever written. Includes letters, historic photographs, maps and more. 528pp. 6⅛ x 9¼. 28587-1 Pa. $12.95

ANCIENT EGYPTIAN MATERIALS AND INDUSTRIES, A. Lucas and J. Harris. Fascinating, comprehensive, thoroughly documented text describes this ancient civilization's vast resources and the processes that incorporated them in daily life, including the use of animal products, building materials, cosmetics, perfumes and incense, fibers, glazed ware, glass and its manufacture, materials used in the mummification process, and much more. 544pp. 6¹⁄₈ x 9¹⁄₄. (USO) 40446-3 Pa. $16.95

RUSSIAN STORIES/PYCCKNE PACCKA3bl: A Dual-Language Book, edited by Gleb Struve. Twelve tales by such masters as Chekhov, Tolstoy, Dostoevsky, Pushkin, others. Excellent word-for-word English translations on facing pages, plus teaching and study aids, Russian/English vocabulary, biographical/critical introductions, more. 416pp. 5⅜ x 8½. 26244-8 Pa. $9.95

PHILADELPHIA THEN AND NOW: 60 Sites Photographed in the Past and Present, Kenneth Finkel and Susan Oyama. Rare photographs of City Hall, Logan Square, Independence Hall, Betsy Ross House, other landmarks juxtaposed with contemporary views. Captures changing face of historic city. Introduction. Captions. 128pp. 8¼ x 11. 25790-8 Pa. $9.95

AIA ARCHITECTURAL GUIDE TO NASSAU AND SUFFOLK COUNTIES, LONG ISLAND, The American Institute of Architects, Long Island Chapter, and the Society for the Preservation of Long Island Antiquities. Comprehensive, well-researched and generously illustrated volume brings to life over three centuries of Long Island's great architectural heritage. More than 240 photographs with authoritative, extensively detailed captions. 176pp. 8¼ x 11. 26946-9 Pa. $14.95

NORTH AMERICAN INDIAN LIFE: Customs and Traditions of 23 Tribes, Elsie Clews Parsons (ed.). 27 fictionalized essays by noted anthropologists examine religion, customs, government, additional facets of life among the Winnebago, Crow, Zuni, Eskimo, other tribes. 480pp. 6⅛ x 9¼. 27377-6 Pa. $10.95

FRANK LLOYD WRIGHT'S DANA HOUSE, Donald Hoffmann. Pictorial essay of residential masterpiece with over 160 interior and exterior photos, plans, elevations, sketches and studies. 128pp. 9¼ x 10¾. 29120-0 Pa. $12.95

THE MALE AND FEMALE FIGURE IN MOTION: 60 Classic Photographic Sequences, Eadweard Muybridge. 60 true-action photographs of men and women walking, running, climbing, bending, turning, etc., reproduced from rare 19th-century masterpiece. vi + 121pp. 9 x 12. 24745-7 Pa. $10.95

1001 QUESTIONS ANSWERED ABOUT THE SEASHORE, N. J. Berrill and Jacquelyn Berrill. Queries answered about dolphins, sea snails, sponges, starfish, fishes, shore birds, many others. Covers appearance, breeding, growth, feeding, much more. 305pp. 5¼ x 8¼. 23366-9 Pa. $9.95

ATTRACTING BIRDS TO YOUR YARD, William J. Weber. Easy-to-follow guide offers advice on how to attract the greatest diversity of birds: birdhouses, feeders, water and waterers, much more. 96pp. 5³⁄₁₆ x 8¼. 28927-3 Pa. $2.50

MEDICINAL AND OTHER USES OF NORTH AMERICAN PLANTS: A Historical Survey with Special Reference to the Eastern Indian Tribes, Charlotte Erichsen-Brown. Chronological historical citations document 500 years of usage of plants, trees, shrubs native to eastern Canada, northeastern U.S. Also complete identifying information. 343 illustrations. 544pp. 6½ x 9¼. 25951-X Pa. $12.95

STORYBOOK MAZES, Dave Phillips. 23 stories and mazes on two-page spreads: Wizard of Oz, Treasure Island, Robin Hood, etc. Solutions. 64pp. 8¼ x 11. 23628-5 Pa. $2.95

AMERICAN NEGRO SONGS: 230 Folk Songs and Spirituals, Religious and Secular, John W. Work. This authoritative study traces the African influences of songs sung and played by black Americans at work, in church, and as entertainment. The author discusses the lyric significance of such songs as "Swing Low, Sweet Chariot," "John Henry," and others and offers the words and music for 230 songs. Bibliography. Index of Song Titles. 272pp. 6¹⁄₂ x 9¹⁄₄. 40271-1 Pa. $9.95

MOVIE-STAR PORTRAITS OF THE FORTIES, John Kobal (ed.). 163 glamor, studio photos of 106 stars of the 1940s: Rita Hayworth, Ava Gardner, Marlon Brando, Clark Gable, many more. 176pp. 8⅜ x 11¼. 23546-7 Pa. $14.95

BENCHLEY LOST AND FOUND, Robert Benchley. Finest humor from early 30s, about pet peeves, child psychologists, post office and others. Mostly unavailable elsewhere. 73 illustrations by Peter Arno and others. 183pp. 5⅜ x 8½. 22410-4 Pa. $6.95

YEKL and THE IMPORTED BRIDEGROOM AND OTHER STORIES OF YIDDISH NEW YORK, Abraham Cahan. Film Hester Street based on Yekl (1896). Novel, other stories among first about Jewish immigrants on N.Y.'s East Side. 240pp. 5⅜ x 8½. 22427-9 Pa. $6.95

SELECTED POEMS, Walt Whitman. Generous sampling from *Leaves of Grass*. Twenty-four poems include "I Hear America Singing," "Song of the Open Road," "I Sing the Body Electric," "When Lilacs Last in the Dooryard Bloom'd," "O Captain! My Captain!"–all reprinted from an authoritative edition. Lists of titles and first lines. 128pp. 5³⁄₁₆ x 8¼. 26878-0 Pa. $1.00

THE BEST TALES OF HOFFMANN, E. T. A. Hoffmann. 10 of Hoffmann's most important stories: "Nutcracker and the King of Mice," "The Golden Flowerpot," etc. 458pp. 5⅜ x 8½. 21793-0 Pa. $9.95

FROM FETISH TO GOD IN ANCIENT EGYPT, E. A. Wallis Budge. Rich detailed survey of Egyptian conception of "God" and gods, magic, cult of animals, Osiris, more. Also, superb English translations of hymns and legends. 240 illustrations. 545pp. 5⅜ x 8½. 25803-3 Pa. $13.95

FRENCH STORIES/CONTES FRANÇAIS: A Dual-Language Book, Wallace Fowlie. Ten stories by French masters, Voltaire to Camus: "Micromegas" by Voltaire; "The Atheist's Mass" by Balzac; "Minuet" by de Maupassant; "The Guest" by Camus, six more. Excellent English translations on facing pages. Also French-English vocabulary list, exercises, more. 352pp. 5⅜ x 8½. 26443-2 Pa. $9.95

CHICAGO AT THE TURN OF THE CENTURY IN PHOTOGRAPHS: 122 Historic Views from the Collections of the Chicago Historical Society, Larry A. Viskochil. Rare large-format prints offer detailed views of City Hall, State Street, the Loop, Hull House, Union Station, many other landmarks, circa 1904-1913. Introduction. Captions. Maps. 144pp. 9⅜ x 12¼. 24656-6 Pa. $12.95

OLD BROOKLYN IN EARLY PHOTOGRAPHS, 1865-1929, William Lee Younger. Luna Park, Gravesend race track, construction of Grand Army Plaza, moving of Hotel Brighton, etc. 157 previously unpublished photographs. 165pp. 8⅞ x 11¾. 23587-4 Pa. $13.95

THE MYTHS OF THE NORTH AMERICAN INDIANS, Lewis Spence. Rich anthology of the myths and legends of the Algonquins, Iroquois, Pawnees and Sioux, prefaced by an extensive historical and ethnological commentary. 36 illustrations. 480pp. 5⅜ x 8½. 25967-6 Pa. $10.95

AN ENCYCLOPEDIA OF BATTLES: Accounts of Over 1,560 Battles from 1479 B.C. to the Present, David Eggenberger. Essential details of every major battle in recorded history from the first battle of Megiddo in 1479 B.C. to Grenada in 1984. List of Battle Maps. New Appendix covering the years 1967-1984. Index. 99 illustrations. 544pp. 6½ x 9¼. 24913-1 Pa. $16.95

SAILING ALONE AROUND THE WORLD, Captain Joshua Slocum. First man to sail around the world, alone, in small boat. One of great feats of seamanship told in delightful manner. 67 illustrations. 294pp. 5⅜ x 8½. 20326-3 Pa. $6.95

ANARCHISM AND OTHER ESSAYS, Emma Goldman. Powerful, penetrating, prophetic essays on direct action, role of minorities, prison reform, puritan hypocrisy, violence, etc. 271pp. 5⅜ x 8½. 22484-8 Pa. $7.95

MYTHS OF THE HINDUS AND BUDDHISTS, Ananda K. Coomaraswamy and Sister Nivedita. Great stories of the epics; deeds of Krishna, Shiva, taken from puranas, Vedas, folk tales; etc. 32 illustrations. 400pp. 5⅜ x 8½. 21759-0 Pa. $12.95

THE TRAUMA OF BIRTH, Otto Rank. Rank's controversial thesis that anxiety neurosis is caused by profound psychological trauma which occurs at birth. 256pp. 5⅜ x 8½. 27974-X Pa. $7.95

A THEOLOGICO-POLITICAL TREATISE, Benedict Spinoza. Also contains unfinished Political Treatise. Great classic on religious liberty, theory of government on common consent. R. Elwes translation. Total of 421pp. 5⅜ x 8½. 20249-6 Pa. $9.95

MY BONDAGE AND MY FREEDOM, Frederick Douglass. Born a slave, Douglass became outspoken force in antislavery movement. The best of Douglass' autobiographies. Graphic description of slave life. 464pp. 5⅜ x 8½. 22457-0 Pa. $8.95

FOLLOWING THE EQUATOR: A Journey Around the World, Mark Twain. Fascinating humorous account of 1897 voyage to Hawaii, Australia, India, New Zealand, etc. Ironic, bemused reports on peoples, customs, climate, flora and fauna, politics, much more. 197 illustrations. 720pp. 5⅜ x 8½. 26113-1 Pa. $15.95

THE PEOPLE CALLED SHAKERS, Edward D. Andrews. Definitive study of Shakers: origins, beliefs, practices, dances, social organization, furniture and crafts, etc. 33 illustrations. 351pp. 5⅜ x 8½. 21081-2 Pa. $8.95

THE MYTHS OF GREECE AND ROME, H. A. Guerber. A classic of mythology, generously illustrated, long prized for its simple, graphic, accurate retelling of the principal myths of Greece and Rome, and for its commentary on their origins and significance. With 64 illustrations by Michelangelo, Raphael, Titian, Rubens, Canova, Bernini and others. 480pp. 5⅜ x 8½. 27584-1 Pa. $9.95

PSYCHOLOGY OF MUSIC, Carl E. Seashore. Classic work discusses music as a medium from psychological viewpoint. Clear treatment of physical acoustics, auditory apparatus, sound perception, development of musical skills, nature of musical feeling, host of other topics. 88 figures. 408pp. 5⅜ x 8½. 21851-1 Pa. $11.95

THE PHILOSOPHY OF HISTORY, Georg W. Hegel. Great classic of Western thought develops concept that history is not chance but rational process, the evolution of freedom. 457pp. 5⅜ x 8½. 20112-0 Pa. $9.95

THE BOOK OF TEA, Kakuzo Okakura. Minor classic of the Orient: entertaining, charming explanation, interpretation of traditional Japanese culture in terms of tea ceremony. 94pp. 5⅜ x 8½. 20070-1 Pa. $3.95

LIFE IN ANCIENT EGYPT, Adolf Erman. Fullest, most thorough, detailed older account with much not in more recent books, domestic life, religion, magic, medicine, commerce, much more. Many illustrations reproduce tomb paintings, carvings, hieroglyphs, etc. 597pp. 5⅜ x 8½. 22632-8 Pa. $12.95

SUNDIALS, Their Theory and Construction, Albert Waugh. Far and away the best, most thorough coverage of ideas, mathematics concerned, types, construction, adjusting anywhere. Simple, nontechnical treatment allows even children to build several of these dials. Over 100 illustrations. 230pp. 5⅜ x 8½. 22947-5 Pa. $8.95

THEORETICAL HYDRODYNAMICS, L. M. Milne-Thomson. Classic exposition of the mathematical theory of fluid motion, applicable to both hydrodynamics and aerodynamics. Over 600 exercises. 768pp. 6⅛ x 9¼. 68970-0 Pa. $20.95

SONGS OF EXPERIENCE: Facsimile Reproduction with 26 Plates in Full Color, William Blake. 26 full-color plates from a rare 1826 edition. Includes "The Tyger," "London," "Holy Thursday," and other poems. Printed text of poems. 48pp. 5¼ x 7. 24636-1 Pa. $4.95

OLD-TIME VIGNETTES IN FULL COLOR, Carol Belanger Grafton (ed.). Over 390 charming, often sentimental illustrations, selected from archives of Victorian graphics—pretty women posing, children playing, food, flowers, kittens and puppies, smiling cherubs, birds and butterflies, much more. All copyright-free. 48pp. 9¼ x 12¼. 27269-9 Pa. $7.95

PERSPECTIVE FOR ARTISTS, Rex Vicat Cole. Depth, perspective of sky and sea, shadows, much more, not usually covered. 391 diagrams, 81 reproductions of drawings and paintings. 279pp. 5⅜ x 8½. 22487-2 Pa. $7.95

DRAWING THE LIVING FIGURE, Joseph Sheppard. Innovative approach to artistic anatomy focuses on specifics of surface anatomy, rather than muscles and bones. Over 170 drawings of live models in front, back and side views, and in widely varying poses. Accompanying diagrams. 177 illustrations. Introduction. Index. 144pp. 8⅜ x11¼. 26723-7 Pa. $8.95

GOTHIC AND OLD ENGLISH ALPHABETS: 100 Complete Fonts, Dan X. Solo. Add power, elegance to posters, signs, other graphics with 100 stunning copyright-free alphabets: Blackstone, Dolbey, Germania, 97 more–including many lower-case, numerals, punctuation marks. 104pp. 8⅛ x 11. 24695-7 Pa. $8.95

HOW TO DO BEADWORK, Mary White. Fundamental book on craft from simple projects to five-bead chains and woven works. 106 illustrations. 142pp. 5⅜ x 8. 20697-1 Pa. $5.95

THE BOOK OF WOOD CARVING, Charles Marshall Sayers. Finest book for beginners discusses fundamentals and offers 34 designs. "Absolutely first rate . . . well thought out and well executed."–E. J. Tangerman. 118pp. 7¾ x 10⅝. 23654-4 Pa. $7.95

ILLUSTRATED CATALOG OF CIVIL WAR MILITARY GOODS: Union Army Weapons, Insignia, Uniform Accessories, and Other Equipment, Schuyler, Hartley, and Graham. Rare, profusely illustrated 1846 catalog includes Union Army uniform and dress regulations, arms and ammunition, coats, insignia, flags, swords, rifles, etc. 226 illustrations. 160pp. 9 x 12. 24939-5 Pa. $10.95

WOMEN'S FASHIONS OF THE EARLY 1900s: An Unabridged Republication of "New York Fashions, 1909," National Cloak & Suit Co. Rare catalog of mail-order fashions documents women's and children's clothing styles shortly after the turn of the century. Captions offer full descriptions, prices. Invaluable resource for fashion, costume historians. Approximately 725 illustrations. 128pp. 8⅜ x 11¼. 27276-1 Pa. $11.95

THE 1912 AND 1915 GUSTAV STICKLEY FURNITURE CATALOGS, Gustav Stickley. With over 200 detailed illustrations and descriptions, these two catalogs are essential reading and reference materials and identification guides for Stickley furniture. Captions cite materials, dimensions and prices. 112pp. 6½ x 9¼. 26676-1 Pa. $9.95

EARLY AMERICAN LOCOMOTIVES, John H. White, Jr. Finest locomotive engravings from early 19th century: historical (1804–74), main-line (after 1870), special, foreign, etc. 147 plates. 142pp. 11⅜ x 8¼. 22772-3 Pa. $10.95

THE TALL SHIPS OF TODAY IN PHOTOGRAPHS, Frank O. Braynard. Lavishly illustrated tribute to nearly 100 majestic contemporary sailing vessels: Amerigo Vespucci, Clearwater, Constitution, Eagle, Mayflower, Sea Cloud, Victory, many more. Authoritative captions provide statistics, background on each ship. 190 black-and-white photographs and illustrations. Introduction. 128pp. 8⅞ x 11¾. 27163-3 Pa. $14.95

LITTLE BOOK OF EARLY AMERICAN CRAFTS AND TRADES, Peter Stockham (ed.). 1807 children's book explains crafts and trades: baker, hatter, cooper, potter, and many others. 23 copperplate illustrations. 140pp. 4⅝ x 6.
23336-7 Pa. $4.95

VICTORIAN FASHIONS AND COSTUMES FROM HARPER'S BAZAR, 1867–1898, Stella Blum (ed.). Day costumes, evening wear, sports clothes, shoes, hats, other accessories in over 1,000 detailed engravings. 320pp. 9⅜ x 12¼.
22990-4 Pa. $15.95

GUSTAV STICKLEY, THE CRAFTSMAN, Mary Ann Smith. Superb study surveys broad scope of Stickley's achievement, especially in architecture. Design philosophy, rise and fall of the Craftsman empire, descriptions and floor plans for many Craftsman houses, more. 86 black-and-white halftones. 31 line illustrations. Introduction 208pp. 6½ x 9¼. 27210-9 Pa. $9.95

THE LONG ISLAND RAIL ROAD IN EARLY PHOTOGRAPHS, Ron Ziel. Over 220 rare photos, informative text document origin (1844) and development of rail service on Long Island. Vintage views of early trains, locomotives, stations, passengers, crews, much more. Captions. 8⅞ x 11¾. 26301-0 Pa. $13.95

VOYAGE OF THE LIBERDADE, Joshua Slocum. Great 19th-century mariner's thrilling, first-hand account of the wreck of his ship off South America, the 35-foot boat he built from the wreckage, and its remarkable voyage home. 128pp. 5⅜ x 8½.
40022-0 Pa. $4.95

TEN BOOKS ON ARCHITECTURE, Vitruvius. The most important book ever written on architecture. Early Roman aesthetics, technology, classical orders, site selection, all other aspects. Morgan translation. 331pp. 5⅜ x 8½. 20645-9 Pa. $8.95

THE HUMAN FIGURE IN MOTION, Eadweard Muybridge. More than 4,500 stopped-action photos, in action series, showing undraped men, women, children jumping, lying down, throwing, sitting, wrestling, carrying, etc. 390pp. 7⅞ x 10⅝.
20204-6 Clothbd. $27.95

TREES OF THE EASTERN AND CENTRAL UNITED STATES AND CANADA, William M. Harlow. Best one-volume guide to 140 trees. Full descriptions, woodlore, range, etc. Over 600 illustrations. Handy size. 288pp. 4½ x 6⅜.
20395-6 Pa. $6.95

SONGS OF WESTERN BIRDS, Dr. Donald J. Borror. Complete song and call repertoire of 60 western species, including flycatchers, juncoes, cactus wrens, many more–includes fully illustrated booklet. Cassette and manual 99913-0 $8.95

GROWING AND USING HERBS AND SPICES, Milo Miloradovich. Versatile handbook provides all the information needed for cultivation and use of all the herbs and spices available in North America. 4 illustrations. Index. Glossary. 236pp. 5⅜ x 8½.
25058-X Pa. $7.95

BIG BOOK OF MAZES AND LABYRINTHS, Walter Shepherd. 50 mazes and labyrinths in all–classical, solid, ripple, and more–in one great volume. Perfect inexpensive puzzler for clever youngsters. Full solutions. 112pp. 8⅛ x 11.
22951-3 Pa. $5.95

PIANO TUNING, J. Cree Fischer. Clearest, best book for beginner, amateur. Simple repairs, raising dropped notes, tuning by easy method of flattened fifths. No previous skills needed. 4 illustrations. 201pp. 5⅜ x 8½. 23267-0 Pa. $6.95

HINTS TO SINGERS, Lillian Nordica. Selecting the right teacher, developing confidence, overcoming stage fright, and many other important skills receive thoughtful discussion in this indispensible guide, written by a world-famous diva of four decades' experience. 96pp. 5⅜ x 8½. 40094-8 Pa. $4.95

THE COMPLETE NONSENSE OF EDWARD LEAR, Edward Lear. All nonsense limericks, zany alphabets, Owl and Pussycat, songs, nonsense botany, etc., illustrated by Lear. Total of 320pp. 5⅜ x 8½. (USO) 20167-8 Pa. $7.95

VICTORIAN PARLOUR POETRY: An Annotated Anthology, Michael R. Turner. 117 gems by Longfellow, Tennyson, Browning, many lesser-known poets. "The Village Blacksmith," "Curfew Must Not Ring Tonight," "Only a Baby Small," dozens more, often difficult to find elsewhere. Index of poets, titles, first lines. xxiii + 325pp. 5⅝ x 8¼. 27044-0 Pa. $8.95

DUBLINERS, James Joyce. Fifteen stories offer vivid, tightly focused observations of the lives of Dublin's poorer classes. At least one, "The Dead," is considered a masterpiece. Reprinted complete and unabridged from standard edition. 160pp. 5$\frac{3}{16}$ x 8¼. 26870-5 Pa. $1.00

GREAT WEIRD TALES: 14 Stories by Lovecraft, Blackwood, Machen and Others, S. T. Joshi (ed.). 14 spellbinding tales, including "The Sin Eater," by Fiona McLeod, "The Eye Above the Mantel," by Frank Belknap Long, as well as renowned works by R. H. Barlow, Lord Dunsany, Arthur Machen, W. C. Morrow and eight other masters of the genre. 256pp. 5⅜ x 8½. (USO) 40436-6 Pa. $8.95

THE BOOK OF THE SACRED MAGIC OF ABRAMELIN THE MAGE, translated by S. MacGregor Mathers. Medieval manuscript of ceremonial magic. Basic document in Aleister Crowley, Golden Dawn groups. 268pp. 5⅜ x 8½. 23211-5 Pa. $9.95

NEW RUSSIAN-ENGLISH AND ENGLISH-RUSSIAN DICTIONARY, M. A. O'Brien. This is a remarkably handy Russian dictionary, containing a surprising amount of information, including over 70,000 entries. 366pp. 4½ x 6⅛. 20208-9 Pa. $10.95

HISTORIC HOMES OF THE AMERICAN PRESIDENTS, Second, Revised Edition, Irvin Haas. A traveler's guide to American Presidential homes, most open to the public, depicting and describing homes occupied by every American President from George Washington to George Bush. With visiting hours, admission charges, travel routes. 175 photographs. Index. 160pp. 8¼ x 11. 26751-2 Pa. $11.95

NEW YORK IN THE FORTIES, Andreas Feininger. 162 brilliant photographs by the well-known photographer, formerly with *Life* magazine. Commuters, shoppers, Times Square at night, much else from city at its peak. Captions by John von Hartz. 181pp. 9¼ x 10¾. 23585-8 Pa. $13.95

INDIAN SIGN LANGUAGE, William Tomkins. Over 525 signs developed by Sioux and other tribes. Written instructions and diagrams. Also 290 pictographs. 111pp. 6⅛ x 9¼. 22029-X Pa. $3.95

CATALOG OF DOVER BOOKS

ANATOMY: A Complete Guide for Artists, Joseph Sheppard. A master of figure drawing shows artists how to render human anatomy convincingly. Over 460 illustrations. 224pp. 8⅜ x 11¼. 27279-6 Pa. $11.95

MEDIEVAL CALLIGRAPHY: Its History and Technique, Marc Drogin. Spirited history, comprehensive instruction manual covers 13 styles (ca. 4th century thru 15th). Excellent photographs; directions for duplicating medieval techniques with modern tools. 224pp. 8⅜ x 11¼. 26142-5 Pa. $12.95

DRIED FLOWERS: How to Prepare Them, Sarah Whitlock and Martha Rankin. Complete instructions on how to use silica gel, meal and borax, perlite aggregate, sand and borax, glycerine and water to create attractive permanent flower arrangements. 12 illustrations. 32pp. 5⅜ x 8½. 21802-3 Pa. $1.00

EASY-TO-MAKE BIRD FEEDERS FOR WOODWORKERS, Scott D. Campbell. Detailed, simple-to-use guide for designing, constructing, caring for and using feeders. Text, illustrations for 12 classic and contemporary designs. 96pp. 5⅜ x 8½. 25847-5 Pa. $3.95

SCOTTISH WONDER TALES FROM MYTH AND LEGEND, Donald A. Mackenzie. 16 lively tales tell of giants rumbling down mountainsides, of a magic wand that turns stone pillars into warriors, of gods and goddesses, evil hags, powerful forces and more. 240pp. 5⅜ x 8½. 29677-6 Pa. $6.95

THE HISTORY OF UNDERCLOTHES, C. Willett Cunnington and Phyllis Cunnington. Fascinating, well-documented survey covering six centuries of English undergarments, enhanced with over 100 illustrations: 12th-century laced-up bodice, footed long drawers (1795), 19th-century bustles, 19th-century corsets for men, Victorian "bust improvers," much more. 272pp. 5⅜ x 8¼. 27124-2 Pa. $9.95

ARTS AND CRAFTS FURNITURE: The Complete Brooks Catalog of 1912, Brooks Manufacturing Co. Photos and detailed descriptions of more than 150 now very collectible furniture designs from the Arts and Crafts movement depict davenports, settees, buffets, desks, tables, chairs, bedsteads, dressers and more, all built of solid, quarter-sawed oak. Invaluable for students and enthusiasts of antiques, Americana and the decorative arts. 80pp. 6½ x 9¼. 27471-3 Pa. $8.95

WILBUR AND ORVILLE: A Biography of the Wright Brothers, Fred Howard. Definitive, crisply written study tells the full story of the brothers' lives and work. A vividly written biography, unparalleled in scope and color, that also captures the spirit of an extraordinary era. 560pp. 6⅛ x 9¼. 40297-5 Pa. $17.95

THE ARTS OF THE SAILOR: Knotting, Splicing and Ropework, Hervey Garrett Smith. Indispensable shipboard reference covers tools, basic knots and useful hitches; handsewing and canvas work, more. Over 100 illustrations. Delightful reading for sea lovers. 256pp. 5⅜ x 8½. 26440-8 Pa. $8.95

FRANK LLOYD WRIGHT'S FALLINGWATER: The House and Its History, Second, Revised Edition, Donald Hoffmann. A total revision–both in text and illustrations–of the standard document on Fallingwater, the boldest, most personal architectural statement of Wright's mature years, updated with valuable new material from the recently opened Frank Lloyd Wright Archives. "Fascinating"–*The New York Times*. 116 illustrations. 128pp. 9¼ x 10¾. 27430-6 Pa. $12.95

PHOTOGRAPHIC SKETCHBOOK OF THE CIVIL WAR, Alexander Gardner. 100 photos taken on field during the Civil War. Famous shots of Manassas Harper's Ferry, Lincoln, Richmond, slave pens, etc. 244pp. 10⅝ x 8¼.   22731-6 Pa. $10.95

FIVE ACRES AND INDEPENDENCE, Maurice G. Kains. Great back-to-the-land classic explains basics of self-sufficient farming. The one book to get. 95 illustrations. 397pp. 5⅜ x 8½.   20974-1 Pa. $7.95

SONGS OF EASTERN BIRDS, Dr. Donald J. Borror. Songs and calls of 60 species most common to eastern U.S.: warblers, woodpeckers, flycatchers, thrushes, larks, many more in high-quality recording.   Cassette and manual 99912-2 $9.95

A MODERN HERBAL, Margaret Grieve. Much the fullest, most exact, most useful compilation of herbal material. Gigantic alphabetical encyclopedia, from aconite to zedoary, gives botanical information, medical properties, folklore, economic uses, much else. Indispensable to serious reader. 161 illustrations. 888pp. 6½ x 9¼. 2-vol. set. (USO)   Vol. I: 22798-7 Pa. $9.95
Vol. II: 22799-5 Pa. $9.95

HIDDEN TREASURE MAZE BOOK, Dave Phillips. Solve 34 challenging mazes accompanied by heroic tales of adventure. Evil dragons, people-eating plants, blood-thirsty giants, many more dangerous adversaries lurk at every twist and turn. 34 mazes, stories, solutions. 48pp. 8¼ x 11.   24566-7 Pa. $2.95

LETTERS OF W. A. MOZART, Wolfgang A. Mozart. Remarkable letters show bawdy wit, humor, imagination, musical insights, contemporary musical world; includes some letters from Leopold Mozart. 276pp. 5⅜ x 8½.   22859-2 Pa. $7.95

BASIC PRINCIPLES OF CLASSICAL BALLET, Agrippina Vaganova. Great Russian theoretician, teacher explains methods for teaching classical ballet. 118 illustrations. 175pp. 5⅜ x 8½.   22036-2 Pa. $5.95

THE JUMPING FROG, Mark Twain. Revenge edition. The original story of The Celebrated Jumping Frog of Calaveras County, a hapless French translation, and Twain's hilarious "retranslation" from the French. 12 illustrations. 66pp. 5⅜ x 8½.   22686-7 Pa. $3.95

BEST REMEMBERED POEMS, Martin Gardner (ed.). The 126 poems in this superb collection of 19th- and 20th-century British and American verse range from Shelley's "To a Skylark" to the impassioned "Renascence" of Edna St. Vincent Millay and to Edward Lear's whimsical "The Owl and the Pussycat." 224pp. 5⅜ x 8½.   27165-X Pa. $5.95

COMPLETE SONNETS, William Shakespeare. Over 150 exquisite poems deal with love, friendship, the tyranny of time, beauty's evanescence, death and other themes in language of remarkable power, precision and beauty. Glossary of archaic terms. 80pp. 5³⁄₁₆ x 8¼.   26686-9 Pa. $1.00

BODIES IN A BOOKSHOP, R. T. Campbell. Challenging mystery of blackmail and murder with ingenious plot and superbly drawn characters. In the best tradition of British suspense fiction. 192pp. 5⅜ x 8½.   24720-1 Pa. $6.95

THE WIT AND HUMOR OF OSCAR WILDE, Alvin Redman (ed.). More than 1,000 ripostes, paradoxes, wisecracks: Work is the curse of the drinking classes; I can resist everything except temptation; etc. 258pp. 5⅜ x 8½.   20602-5 Pa. $6.95

SHAKESPEARE LEXICON AND QUOTATION DICTIONARY, Alexander Schmidt. Full definitions, locations, shades of meaning in every word in plays and poems. More than 50,000 exact quotations. 1,485pp. 6½ x 9¼. 2-vol. set.
Vol. 1: 22726-X Pa. $17.95
Vol. 2: 22727-8 Pa. $17.95

SELECTED POEMS, Emily Dickinson. Over 100 best-known, best-loved poems by one of America's foremost poets, reprinted from authoritative early editions. No comparable edition at this price. Index of first lines. 64pp. 5³⁄₁₆ x 8¼.
26466-1 Pa. $1.00

THE INSIDIOUS DR. FU-MANCHU, Sax Rohmer. The first of the popular mystery series introduces a pair of English detectives to their archnemesis, the diabolical Dr. Fu-Manchu. Flavorful atmosphere, fast-paced action, and colorful characters enliven this classic of the genre. 208pp. 5³⁄₁₆ x 8¼.   29898-1 Pa. $2.00

THE MALLEUS MALEFICARUM OF KRAMER AND SPRENGER, translated by Montague Summers. Full text of most important witchhunter's "bible," used by both Catholics and Protestants. 278pp. 6⅝ x 10.   22802-9 Pa. $12.95

SPANISH STORIES/CUENTOS ESPAÑOLES: A Dual-Language Book, Angel Flores (ed.). Unique format offers 13 great stories in Spanish by Cervantes, Borges, others. Faithful English translations on facing pages. 352pp. 5⅜ x 8½.
25399-6 Pa. $8.95

GARDEN CITY, LONG ISLAND, IN EARLY PHOTOGRAPHS, 1869–1919, Mildred H. Smith. Handsome treasury of 118 vintage pictures, accompanied by carefully researched captions, document the Garden City Hotel fire (1899), the Vanderbilt Cup Race (1908), the first airmail flight departing from the Nassau Boulevard Aerodrome (1911), and much more. 96pp. 8⅞ x 11¾.   40669-5 Pa. $12.95

OLD QUEENS, N.Y., IN EARLY PHOTOGRAPHS, Vincent F. Seyfried and William Asadorian. Over 160 rare photographs of Maspeth, Jamaica, Jackson Heights, and other areas. Vintage views of DeWitt Clinton mansion, 1939 World's Fair and more. Captions. 192pp. 8⅞ x 11.   26358-4 Pa. $12.95

CAPTURED BY THE INDIANS: 15 Firsthand Accounts, 1750-1870, Frederick Drimmer. Astounding true historical accounts of grisly torture, bloody conflicts, relentless pursuits, miraculous escapes and more, by people who lived to tell the tale. 384pp. 5⅜ x 8½.   24901-8 Pa. $8.95

THE WORLD'S GREAT SPEECHES (Fourth Enlarged Edition), Lewis Copeland, Lawrence W. Lamm, and Stephen J. McKenna. Nearly 300 speeches provide public speakers with a wealth of updated quotes and inspiration–from Pericles' funeral oration and William Jennings Bryan's "Cross of Gold Speech" to Malcolm X's powerful words on the Black Revolution and Earl of Spenser's tribute to his sister, Diana, Princess of Wales. 944pp. 5⅜ x 8⅜.   40903-1 Pa. $15.95

THE BOOK OF THE SWORD, Sir Richard F. Burton. Great Victorian scholar/adventurer's eloquent, erudite history of the "queen of weapons"–from prehistory to early Roman Empire. Evolution and development of early swords, variations (sabre, broadsword, cutlass, scimitar, etc.), much more. 336pp. 6⅛ x 9¼.
25434-8 Pa. $9.95

AUTOBIOGRAPHY: The Story of My Experiments with Truth, Mohandas K. Gandhi. Boyhood, legal studies, purification, the growth of the Satyagraha (nonviolent protest) movement. Critical, inspiring work of the man responsible for the freedom of India. 480pp. 5⅜ x 8½. (USO) 24593-4 Pa. $8.95

CELTIC MYTHS AND LEGENDS, T. W. Rolleston. Masterful retelling of Irish and Welsh stories and tales. Cuchulain, King Arthur, Deirdre, the Grail, many more. First paperback edition. 58 full-page illustrations. 512pp. 5⅜ x 8½. 26507-2 Pa. $9.95

THE PRINCIPLES OF PSYCHOLOGY, William James. Famous long course complete, unabridged. Stream of thought, time perception, memory, experimental methods; great work decades ahead of its time. 94 figures. 1,391pp. 5⅜ x 8½. 2-vol. set.
Vol. I: 20381-6 Pa. $13.95
Vol. II: 20382-4 Pa. $14.95

THE WORLD AS WILL AND REPRESENTATION, Arthur Schopenhauer. Definitive English translation of Schopenhauer's life work, correcting more than 1,000 errors, omissions in earlier translations. Translated by E. F. J. Payne. Total of 1,269pp. 5⅜ x 8½. 2-vol. set. Vol. 1: 21761-2 Pa. $12.95
Vol. 2: 21762-0 Pa. $12.95

MAGIC AND MYSTERY IN TIBET, Madame Alexandra David-Neel. Experiences among lamas, magicians, sages, sorcerers, Bonpa wizards. A true psychic discovery. 32 illustrations. 321pp. 5⅜ x 8½. (USO) 22682-4 Pa. $9.95

THE EGYPTIAN BOOK OF THE DEAD, E. A. Wallis Budge. Complete reproduction of Ani's papyrus, finest ever found. Full hieroglyphic text, interlinear transliteration, word-for-word translation, smooth translation. 533pp. 6½ x 9¼.
21866-X Pa. $11.95

MATHEMATICS FOR THE NONMATHEMATICIAN, Morris Kline. Detailed, college-level treatment of mathematics in cultural and historical context, with numerous exercises. Recommended Reading Lists. Tables. Numerous figures. 641pp. 5⅜ x 8½.
24823-2 Pa. $11.95

PROBABILISTIC METHODS IN THE THEORY OF STRUCTURES, Isaac Elishakoff. Well-written introduction covers the elements of the theory of probability from two or more random variables, the reliability of such multivariable structures, the theory of random function, Monte Carlo methods of treating problems incapable of exact solution, and more. Examples. 502pp. 5³/₈ x 8¹/₂. 40691-1 Pa. $16.95

THE RIME OF THE ANCIENT MARINER, Gustave Doré, S. T. Coleridge. Doré's finest work; 34 plates capture moods, subtleties of poem. Flawless full-size reproductions printed on facing pages with authoritative text of poem. "Beautiful. Simply beautiful."–*Publisher's Weekly.* 77pp. 9¼ x 12. 22305-1 Pa. $7.95

NORTH AMERICAN INDIAN DESIGNS FOR ARTISTS AND CRAFTSPEOPLE, Eva Wilson. Over 360 authentic copyright-free designs adapted from Navajo blankets, Hopi pottery, Sioux buffalo hides, more. Geometrics, symbolic figures, plant and animal motifs, etc. 128pp. 8⅜ x 11. (EUK) 25341-4 Pa. $8.95

SCULPTURE: Principles and Practice, Louis Slobodkin. Step-by-step approach to clay, plaster, metals, stone; classical and modern. 253 drawings, photos. 255pp. 8⅛ x 11.
22960-2 Pa. $11.95

THE INFLUENCE OF SEA POWER UPON HISTORY, 1660–1783, A. T. Mahan. Influential classic of naval history and tactics still used as text in war colleges. First paperback edition. 4 maps. 24 battle plans. 640pp. 5⅜ x 8½. 25509-3 Pa. $14.95

THE STORY OF THE TITANIC AS TOLD BY ITS SURVIVORS, Jack Winocour (ed.). What it was really like. Panic, despair, shocking inefficiency, and a little heroism. More thrilling than any fictional account. 26 illustrations. 320pp. 5⅜ x 8½. 20610-6 Pa. $8.95

FAIRY AND FOLK TALES OF THE IRISH PEASANTRY, William Butler Yeats (ed.). Treasury of 64 tales from the twilight world of Celtic myth and legend: "The Soul Cages," "The Kildare Pooka," "King O'Toole and his Goose," many more. Introduction and Notes by W. B. Yeats. 352pp. 5⅜ x 8½. 26941-8 Pa. $8.95

BUDDHIST MAHAYANA TEXTS, E. B. Cowell and Others (eds.). Superb, accurate translations of basic documents in Mahayana Buddhism, highly important in history of religions. The Buddha-karita of Asvaghosha, Larger Sukhavativyuha, more. 448pp. 5⅜ x 8½. 25552-2 Pa. $12.95

ONE TWO THREE . . . INFINITY: Facts and Speculations of Science, George Gamow. Great physicist's fascinating, readable overview of contemporary science: number theory, relativity, fourth dimension, entropy, genes, atomic structure, much more. 128 illustrations. Index. 352pp. 5⅜ x 8½. 25664-2 Pa. $8.95

EXPERIMENTATION AND MEASUREMENT, W. J. Youden. Introductory manual explains laws of measurement in simple terms and offers tips for achieving accuracy and minimizing errors. Mathematics of measurement, use of instruments, experimenting with machines. 1994 edition. Foreword. Preface. Introduction. Epilogue. Selected Readings. Glossary. Index. Tables and figures. 128pp. 5³/₈ x 8¹/₂. 40451-X Pa. $6.95

DALÍ ON MODERN ART: The Cuckolds of Antiquated Modern Art, Salvador Dalí. Influential painter skewers modern art and its practitioners. Outrageous evaluations of Picasso, Cézanne, Turner, more. 15 renderings of paintings discussed. 44 calligraphic decorations by Dalí. 96pp. 5⅜ x 8½. (USO) 29220-7 Pa. $5.95

ANTIQUE PLAYING CARDS: A Pictorial History, Henry René D'Allemagne. Over 900 elaborate, decorative images from rare playing cards (14th–20th centuries): Bacchus, death, dancing dogs, hunting scenes, royal coats of arms, players cheating, much more. 96pp. 9¼ x 12¼. 29265-7 Pa. $12.95

MAKING FURNITURE MASTERPIECES: 30 Projects with Measured Drawings, Franklin H. Gottshall. Step-by-step instructions, illustrations for constructing handsome, useful pieces, among them a Sheraton desk, Chippendale chair, Spanish desk, Queen Anne table and a William and Mary dressing mirror. 224pp. 8⅛ x 11¼. 29338-6 Pa. $13.95

THE FOSSIL BOOK: A Record of Prehistoric Life, Patricia V. Rich et al. Profusely illustrated definitive guide covers everything from single-celled organisms and dinosaurs to birds and mammals and the interplay between climate and man. Over 1,500 illustrations. 760pp. 7½ x 10⅛. 29371-8 Pa. $29.95

Prices subject to change without notice.

Available at your book dealer or write for free catalog to Dept. GI, Dover Publications, Inc., 31 East 2nd St., Mineola, N.Y. 11501. Dover publishes more than 500 books each year on science, elementary and advanced mathematics, biology, music, art, literary history, social sciences and other areas.